A COOK'S DICTIONARY

FIDO

cooking

A COOK'S DICTIONARY

BY HENRY BEARD
& ROY McKIE

WORKMAN PUBLISHING
NEW YORK

 Published simultaneously in Canada by Saunders of Toronto, Inc.

Library of Congress Cataloging in Publication Data

Beard, Henry.
Cooking: a cook's dictionary.

1. Cookery—Dictionaries—Anecdotes, facetiae, satire, etc.
I. McKie, Roy. II. Title.
TX349.B36 1985 640'.207 84-40678
ISBN 0-89480-843-5

Workman Publishing Company
1 West 39 Street
New York, New York 10018

First printing April 1985

Manufactured in the United States of America

10 9 8 7 6 5 4 3 2 1

To Monsieur Boulanger,
proprietor of the first restaurant,
this book is gratefully dedicated.

Acorn

A

Acorn	Somewhat bitter, difficult-to-prepare nut widely eaten by the prehistoric ancestors of modern man before language developed sufficiently to include the phrase "Waiter, take this back and bring me a hamburger."
Aïoli	A rich, extremely garlicky mayonnaise made from olive oil, egg yolks, and about a dozen garlic cloves. Its name derives from an old Provençal word uttered by individuals who had occasion to come into contact with the breath of a person who had just eaten some. For this reason, it is also sometimes known in the south of France as "Aiyiyi," "Oooôogue," "Blèuh," and "Aàáàáàáàágh."
À la	French culinary term meaning "in the style of." Some common preparations that use this prefix are: à la carte (served with a large bill); à l'américaine (served with a faint sneer); a l'ancienne (served with thinly disguised leftovers); à la bourgeoise (served with a Marxist tract embedded in aspic); à la grecque (served by a waiter wearing a dirty apron); à l'italienne (served after a two-hour wait); and à la maître d'hôtel (served at a table next to the kitchen).
Al Dente	Italian term for the desired stage in the preparation of pasta, when it is cooked yet still firm to the bite. Pasta that has been boiled too long is described, according to the degree to which it has been overcooked, as al gummo, al musho, al botcho, and al garbaggio.
Antipasto	Italian-style appetizer.
Antipesto	Fast-growing organization dedicated to the eradication from home and restaurant menus of an overused Genovese sauce based on basil, pine nuts, cheese, garlic, and olive oil.

Appetite	Irresistible longing for an unavailable food.
Apple	Fruit used in salads and desserts. There were once hundreds of varieties of apples, but mass production has reduced the number available to a few bland, easy-to-process hybrids like the Golden Delicious and Red Delicious. Other common commercial apples include the Basketbaldwin, a huge, semisoft, somewhat mealy fruit useful for making apple sludge and holding doors open; the Northern Insippin, a doughy reddish globe with a flavor something like library paste; the Macadam or Tarmac, a slightly oily, gritty apple with handy ridges along the top and bottom that make it very good for throwing at dogs; and the Waterproof Macintosh, which has a nearly impervious quarter-inch skin and rubbery flesh that tastes vaguely of Scotchgard.
Apricot	Delicious, delicately flavored fruit which, due to its susceptibility to spoilage in shipping, is, alas, rarely available fresh and is generally consumed in dried or canned form.
Apricot Brandy	Appropriate liqueur to drink in liberal amounts while contemplating the tragic unavailability of fresh apricots.
Arab Coffee	Thick, black, bitter coffee, traditionally served in tiny cups at gunpoint.
Aroma	A smell described by a bore.
Artichoke	Rather peculiar foodstuff related to the thistle. Artichokes are quite troublesome to eat, but in some ways they are the ideal green vegetable because not only is it unnecessary to finish them, it is entirely proper to leave large portions of them completely untouched.

Appetite

Avoirdupois

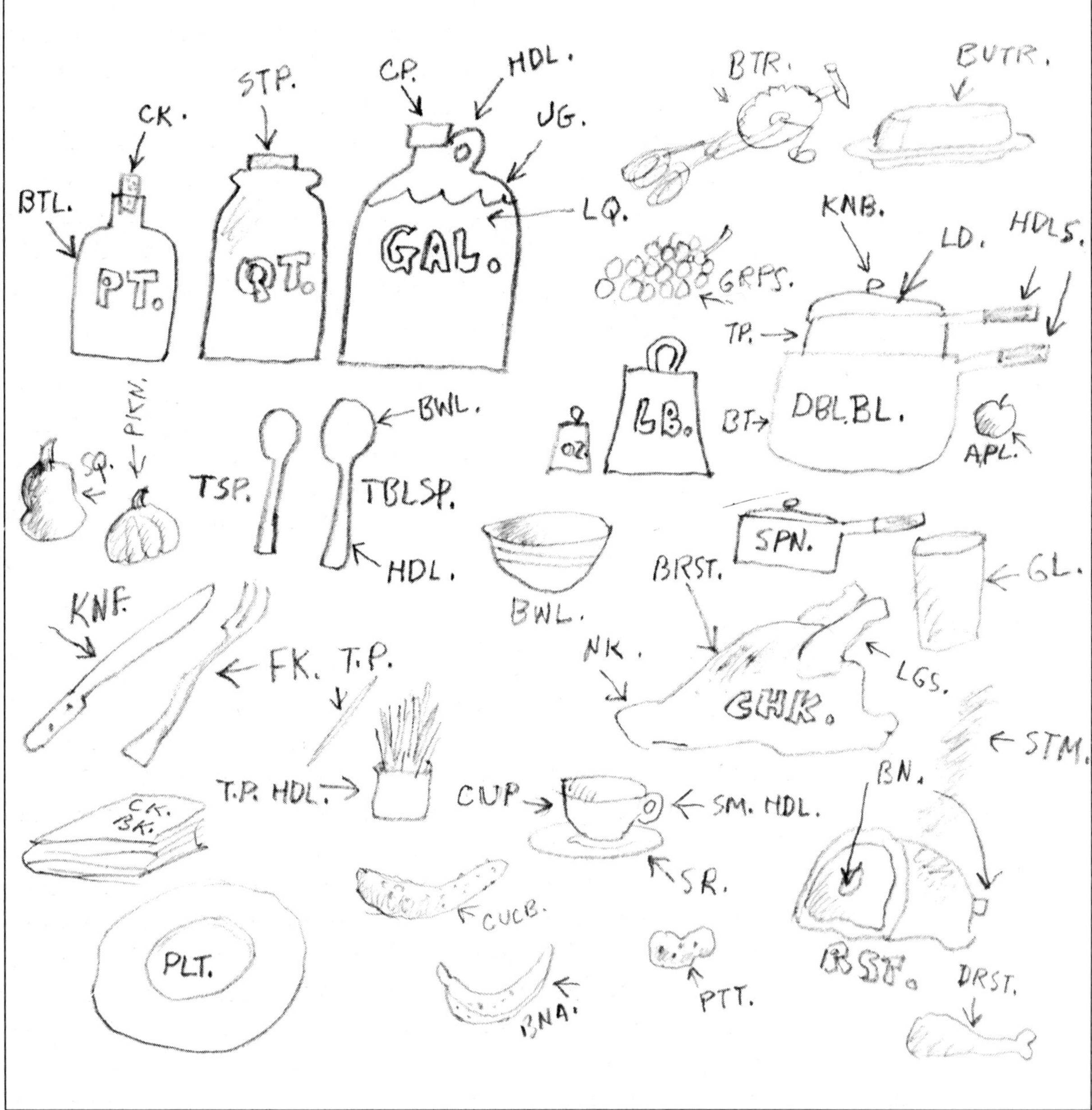

Asparagus

This universally loved vegetable is, paradoxically, the source of a number of tiresome controversies, such as whether the green, purple, or white varieties are the finest; whether it should be cooked standing up or horizontally; whether it should be steamed or lightly poached; whether the stems should be snapped off or cut off and the remainder of the stalks should be peeled; and whether it is acceptable to eat asparagus with the fingers. For this reason, cooks who are expecting disputatious guests are urged to serve Brussels sprouts, which are universally conceded to be unappealing no matter how they are prepared.

Avocado

Tasty, creamy-textured tropical or subtropical fruit. Avocados are the key ingredient in guacamole, one of the many delightful dishes from south of the border that are a major positive contribution to American cuisine and go a long way toward making up for Mexico's one significant negative contribution: Texas.

Avoirdupois

Formal name for the pounds-and-ounces weight system. Metric conversion has gone somewhat slowly in the United States, but dieters should consider an immediate partial changeover to metric units since anyone who now must concede with some embarrassment that he weighs "oh, a bit over 200" could, using kilograms, remark with confidence that he tips the scales at 124. A word of warning, however: other metric measurements are far less satisfactory. A waistline of 39 inches is 99 centimeters, a food containing 100 calories is packed with over 400 kilojoules, and an earnest weight-watcher who jogs 2 miles a day would have to run over 3 kilometers to achieve the same exercise value.

B

Bacon

Salted and smoked meat from the back and sides of a pig. The proper term for a slab of bacon is a gammon or a flitch, and a serving is a rasher or a collop. A person who cooks bacon is a stingfinger or skinflinch. A woman who complains about the cooking smell is a whifftrollop, and one who is enraged by the cost of bacon is a mammongnasher. An individual who takes a freshly cooked piece of bacon without asking is a filch, someone who reveals the identity of such a person is a snacksnatchsnitch, and a cook who punishes him is a snitchbasher. Burnt bacon is called goddamon, and whoever has the chore of cleaning the pan is a bangskillet, potwollop, or pandamner.

Bagel

A round, hard, doughnut-shaped bakery product introduced to America by Jewish immigrants. The derivation of the Yiddish word is uncertain. Some possible sources are: *beygul* (an encounter with the devil early in the morning); *baygal* (to feel like one has a weasel in his stomach); *beykil* (a mouthful of flannel); *bikkel* (to eat one's luggage); and *bakul* (a brick with a hole in it).

Baked Alaska

Extremely challenging dish that consists of ice cream placed on top of sponge cake, covered with beaten egg whites, then baked in an oven at high heat. Because of the trickiness of this recipe, cooks are advised to attempt more modest desserts such as Baked Iowa (jelly beans on a slice of fruit cake with marshmallow sauce); Baked New Jersey (a Mars Bar on a Twinkie topped with Cool Whip); Baked California (goat cheese on a slab of tofu with a yogurt topping); or Baked Connecticut (cream cheese on a piece of pound cake frosted with coconut shreds).

Bacon

Baked Potato — Soft, edible container in which sour cream, melted butter, bacon bits, and chives are served.

Baking — Messy but reliable method of taking a complete kitchen inventory by removing and covering with a sticky batter every single utensil, implement, and container from every drawer, hook, cabinet, or shelf in the kitchen.

Baking Powder — A combination of bicarbonate of soda ($NaHCO_3$) and two acids, calcium acid phosphate ($Ca_3[PO_4]_2$) and sodium aluminum sulfate ($Al_2[SO_4]_3Na_2SO_4$), which when mixed with water and subjected to heat produce carbon dioxide (CO_2), which causes dough to rise. Too much baking powder makes baked products bitter (PhO_2O_3Ey). Too little makes them hard as a rock (O_2UCh).

Barbecue — Primitive summertime rite at which spirits are present, hunks of meat are sacrificed by being burnt on braziers by sauce-smeared men wearing odd hats and aprons with cabalistic slogans, and human flesh is offered to insects.

Basting — Process through which cooking juices in a roasting pan are carefully transferred with a basting siphon, ladle, or spoon to the oven rack, the bottom of the oven, the inside of the oven door, the floor, the stove top, and the counter.

Beans — Edible seed pods of leguminous plants such as kidney beans, lima beans, black beans, and chickpeas. Although their high starch content can produce severe flatulence, beans are very nutritious and are easy to dry and store for long periods of time. Consequently, they were one of the first foods to be domesticated by man and appear in every ancient language including Latin (*detonatae*), Greek (*blammos*), Egyptian (*kerak*), Sanskrit (*fut*), Hindi (*bangha*), Chinese (*qa-pao*), Norse (*frjap*), and Old German (*blatte*).

Barbecue

Beef

The meat of mature cows, bulls, oxen, or steers. The U.S. Department of Agriculture rates beef based on its color, firmness, texture, and fat content, and all inspected sides of beef are marked with a stamp placing them in one of eight categories of declining quality and price: Prime, Choice, and Good are applied to meat that is sold fresh in retail markets; Standard, Commercial, Utility, Cutter, and Canner refer to cuts processed into stews, sauces, and other prepared products found on grocery store shelves. As demand for all kinds of beef has fallen off and costs of production have risen, meat producers have been pressing for the reclassification of beef into a new system with 15 grades: Splendid, Great, Excellent, Royal, Superior, Superb, Sterling, Select, Elite, Aristocrat, Prize, Supreme, Optimum, Other, and None of Your Business.

Beer Cookery

Beer has long been a favored cooking ingredient in the cuisines of Belgium, Britain, and Germany, the best-known producers of the malt-and-hop-based beverage and the innovators of legendary beer-based dishes like carbonnade, Welsh rabbit, and beer soup. In recent years, beer cookery has caught on in America, particularly in the following classic recipe:

HOT DOGS WITH BEER

Two frankfurters
Two frankfurter rolls
Mustard, relishes, and sauerkraut (to taste)
One six-pack of beer

1. Boil the frankfurters, place in lightly toasted rolls, and top with desired condiments.

2. Eat the hot dogs.

3. Drink the beer.

Beef

Bread

Bind

1. (v.) To hold together certain loose foods—delicate little meat dumplings, for example—by adding eggs, flour, or some similar substance which, when heated, causes them to cohere. *2. (n.)* A predicament, such as a cook encounters when he has added too many eggs or too much flour to the delicate little meat dumplings and must decide whether to serve them on a plate or with a tennis racket.

Bird's Nest

The nest of a type of Asian swift or swallow, composed largely of the creature's saliva and used as the chief constituent of the highly prized Chinese dish, Bird's Nest Soup. This dish is of interest to American cooks principally for its importance as a weight-reduction tool, since just thinking about it is sufficient to curb even the heartiest appetite.

Blender

Very handy electric appliance used for making sauces and toppings and for preparing large quantities of daiquiris to serve to guests before dinner if a sauce or topping fails to bind properly, tastes like mud, or smells like livestock dip.

Bread

Many people derive a great deal of satisfaction from baking their own bread, and some psychologists recommend it as a form of therapy since kneading the dough releases tension, the wonderful aroma of freshly baked bread produces a healthy sense of well-being, and the approbation received from family members and friends for serving a much appreciated food builds self-respect. However, some individuals are susceptible to bread mania or rapture of the yeast, and if an acquaintance or loved one purchases a bread truck, interrupts family viewing of television programs with impromptu advertisements for his products, or pesters neighbors for product endorsements, professional help should be sought at once.

Breakfast

Breakfast	A meal without dessert, eaten without wine, and served on a table without a tablecloth. It is best slept through.
Broccoli	One of the very few green vegetables that is invariably available in northern markets during the winter months and one that stores always seem to have an unending supply of. For this reason, "They ran out of it" or "I didn't see any" is not an advisable excuse to offer to a spouse who put it at the top of the shopping list. Much better is "Didn't you read the article on broccolosis?" or "There was an accident on the road, and I had the presence of mind to soak the broccoli heads in gasoline and use them as improvised highway emergency flares."
Broiling	Complicated, multipart cooking method used to give meats a charred exterior and a red or pink interior. There are 12 basic steps to the complete process: spitting, splattering, sticking, smoking, singeing, and scorching, and soaking, sudsing, scraping, scouring, scrubbing, and swearing.
Broth	Soup of concentrated fish or meat stock, and the dish too many cooks spoiled in the old adage from which, by the way, comes the correct term for a collection of cooking professionals: an excess of chefs. Similar terms of interest to the home cook include: a contradiction of cookbooks, a mess of bowls, a panic of sauces, a substitution of spices, a juggle of portions, a tarry of guests, and an astonishment of dirty dishes.
Brunch	Term derived from combining the words "*br*eakfast" and "l*unch*" and used to describe a lavish, buffet-style meal usually served at midday on Sunday, during which gluttons and lushes (glushes) eat and drink too much (gobbuzzle), then fall asleep in the middle of a conversation (chatnap).

Butcher Block

1. Hardwood chopping block or counter surface. *2.* Obscure mental condition that causes some purveyors of meat to describe a portion of a cow's hoof as prime sirloin steak.

Butter

Natural cooking product made from churned milk. Butter is a delicious and essential part of good cuisine, both as a cooking medium and as a sauce constituent, and it is thus distressing that doctors counsel its near total elimination from our diets for reasons of health. It should be noted, however, that whatever the ill effects of long-term butter consumption may be, they pale in comparison to the impact on the blood pressure of being kept waiting for an hour and a half in a physician's outer office with the July 1971 issue of *National Geographic* while he discusses the tuning of his Maserati with his mechanic, or the severe shock to the heart caused by receiving his bill.

C

Cabbage

This soggy, foul-smelling vegetable is almost always shunned by the otherwise knowledgeable cook, and that's a pity because it makes an ideal dinner party side dish. For one thing, it's certain that no one will have some classic recipe to one-up you with, since cabbage is just not the sort of foodstuff that attracts fashionable culinary experimentation; second, the presence of a bowl of thoroughly cooked cabbage on the dining table has the welcome effect of focusing appreciative attention on the remaining courses, no matter how humble or casually prepared they may be; third, a little goes a long way (figure about one pound of cabbage for 70 people, if they're hearty eaters); fourth, the

Butcher Block (1.)

Cake

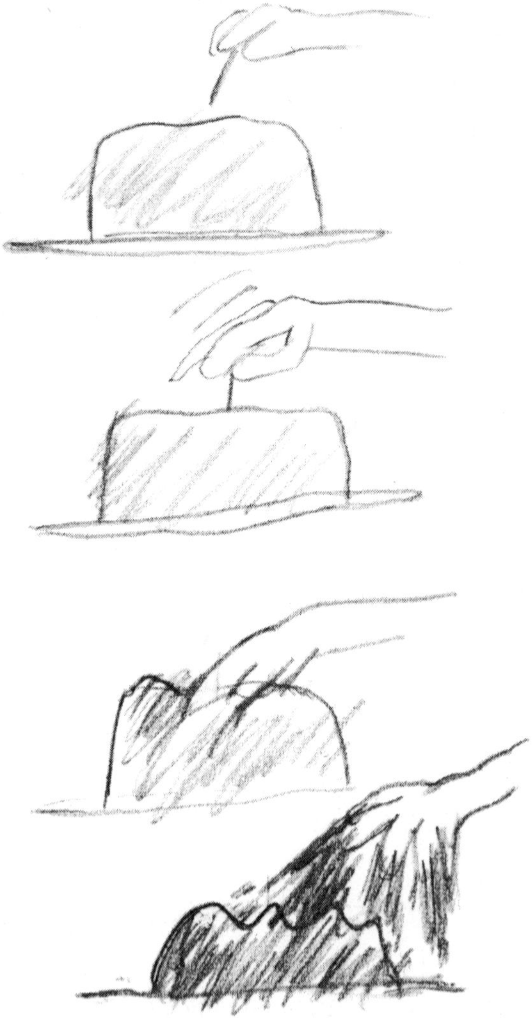

aroma produced by the cooking process seems to discourage guests from tarrying in the house in which it was prepared; and finally, there are no leftovers to contend with—not because there are no leftovers, God knows, but because there is never the slightest hesitation about immediately disposing of them.

Cake

There are two basic types of cakes familiar to the home chef: Strange and Dismal. Which of the two emerges from the oven depends on whether the pan was too large or too small; whether the oven temperature was too high or too low; whether the cake was baked for too long or too short a time; whether the dough was underbeaten or overbeaten; and whether too much or too little sugar, flour, or baking powder was used. A third type, Perfect, is available in pastry shops.

Calorie

Basic measure of the amount of rationalization offered by the average individual prior to taking a second helping of a particular food.

Camembert

Delicate and delicious soft-ripened French cheese. There are easily a thousand different kinds of cheese, and since they vary enormously in appearance and flavor, they are customarily identified by their place in each of three separate categories. The first is type of milk: cow's milk (Brie), goat's milk (chevre), ewe's milk (pecorino), and milk of magnesia (American cheese). The second is texture: spoon (cottage cheese), butterknife (Boursault), fork (Gourmandise), knife (Swiss), cleaver (Cheddar), hatchet (aged Gouda), and chainsaw (parmigiano-reggiano). The third is aroma: yawn (processed cheese), sniff (goat cheese), nose twitch (Roquefort), sneeze (Muenster), grimace (Stilton), gasp (Liederkranz), and stampede (Limburger).

Candle — *1.* A light that makes a mess. *2.* A mess that gives off light.

Carving — Laborious method of producing a meat or poultry hash right at the table.

Cauliflower — A close relative of broccoli and one of the few white vegetables. Because of its unique hue, it is often included in aesthetically pleasing but somewhat ambitious all-white meals consisting, typically, of peeled and boiled new potatoes, pearl onions, creamed cauliflower, and sole with white sauce, served with a Chablis. In practice, of course, most cooks find all-black meals a good deal easier to prepare, and since these repasts obtain their coloration not from the original appearance of the ingredients, but rather from an unintentionally prolonged cooking process at too high a heat, cauliflower may be featured in them as well.

Cereal — The cultivated, edible seeds of domesticated grasses, including wheat, rice, corn, barley, oats, rye, millet, and sorghum. In ancient mythology, Pluto, the god of death, kidnapped Demeter, goddess of agriculture (Ceres to the Romans; hence, "cereal"), and took her to the underworld, thus causing winter. He left behind her unpleasant half-sister, Farina, who provided oatmeal for the starving mortals. Desperate for a change of diet, one young woman, Pandemonia (Casserola in the Latin version), prayed to Phyllo, the god of snacks, for something decent to eat. He gave her a covered dish, warning her not to open it no matter how hungry she became. Driven mad by the prospect of another bowl of cream of wheat, she snatched off the lid and to her horror out flew late guests, burnt fingers, scorched pans, failed mayonnaise, gummy rice, and Greek restaurants. But the container also held the secret for turning leftovers into tasty meals and, since the gods were notoriously fickle,

Carving

Chicken

those little paper doodads that go on the ends of lamb chops. Incidentally, according to legend, Casserola later married Linoleum, the father of the kitchen floor, and had two children of importance to cooks, Ajax and Lysol.

Chef	Any cook who swears in French.
Chicken	Versatile, reasonably priced, easy-to-prepare fowl whose regular appearance on home menus causes it to be greeted with scorn by family members. Oddly enough, the flesh of many exotic animals, such as frogs, terrapins, alligators, small rodents, odd birds, and even insects is invariably described to hesitant diners as tasting just like chicken. This striking coincidence presents an opportunity for creative cooks to vary a monotonous chicken diet at no cost and with very little effort by presenting suitably disguised chicken parts as rare and unique taste treats. A word of advice, however: a few easily acquired props, such as one or two peacock feathers, a tortoise shell, a spring-loaded animal trap, and some outlandish cookbooks, should be left out on the kitchen counter to be spotted by the nosy, and the recipe itself should be made unrecognizable since presenting "cottonmouth" à la king, "turtle" salad sandwiches, "swan" cacciatore, "crocodile" croquettes, or "muskrat" pot pies will tend to undercut the deception.
Chili	Extremely hot-tasting plant of the genus *Capsicum*, usually added in powdered form to a dish made of shredded cattle.
Chili con Carne	Incendiary dogfood widely eaten in Texas.
Chili Parlor	A fistfight at which cooked beef is served.
Chipped Beef on Toast	The only known dish to be specifically outlawed by the Geneva Convention.

Chocolate

Delightful substance derived from the cacao bean. The word "chocolate" comes from its discoverers, the Aztecs of pre-Columbian Mexico, whose name for it in their native Nahuatl was *chocolatl*. Other Aztec words that have contributed to the language of western food are *tomatl*, *avocatl*, and *tamalli*, and *stomachachl*, *Maaloxl*, and *Lomotl*.

Citrus Fruits

Lemons, limes, oranges, grapefruit, and other members of the citrus family. When cut or squeezed, these indispensable fruits exude a juice containing citric acid, a useful substance that helps cooks to quickly locate temporarily misplaced cuts, nicks, and abrasions on their fingers.

Clam Knife

Tricky kitchen tool whose use invariably results in palm readers being able to tell at a glance that a given individual has recently been attempting to open clams.

Cod

Important North Atlantic commercial fish that was once a mainstay of the diets of northeastern Americans but is now served primarily in cake form as an institutional food, particularly at boarding schools and colleges. Its dramatic effect on young men who were fed it once a week is reflected in such books as *Cod, Graves, and Scholars*, *Cod and Man at Yale*, and *The Cod That Failed*.

Coffee

Stimulating beverage brewed from the roasted, ground beans of the coffee plant. Coffee contains caffeine, a rather powerful alkaloid substance, excess consumption of which can result in restlessness, tension, and hyperactivity. If you find that you have an urge to collect your recipes, clean out your freezer, alphabetize your spice rack, or reorganize your pots and pans according to the musical tone they emit when struck with a spoon, you are probably drinking too much coffee.

Cookbook

Colas	Sweet, carbonated beverages. In some states these and other soft drinks are now sold in deposit containers, but the minor inconvenience of return trips to the place of purchase can be mitigated by combining them with the routine visits to the tailor and the dentist necessitated by regular consumption of their contents.
Complaint	Expression of dissatisfaction made to a chef or cook, e.g., "This food stinks."
Compliment	Expression of approval made to a chef or cook, e.g., "This food stinks, but I love your plates."
Condiment	An accompaniment to food, such as salt, pepper, ketchup, mustard, relish, or hot sauce. Unlike seasonings, which are added to foods in excessive amounts in the kitchen, condiments are served at the table so that each individual diner can put on his or her portion the precise amount necessary to make it unpalatable.
Cookbook	A collection of recipes arranged in such a fashion that the cook must turn the page just after the point where a thick paste of flour, water, and lard is mixed by hand.
Cookie Sheet	*1.* Thin, flat rectangular piece of metal used for baking cookies in an oven. *2.* Type of crumb-covered linen found on beds of individuals whose midnight snacks are eaten between the covers.
Cookware	Informal term for utensils in which foods are heated. There are many different brands, but there are only seven basic types: heavy/messy (cast-iron); clumsy/hefty (stainless-steel); costly/silly (copper); flimsy/junky (aluminum); clunky/bulky (enamel); dopey/crazy (glass); and icky/phooey (Teflon-coated).

Corkscrew

There are several tools of different designs for removing corks from wine bottles, but the ones most commonly found in kitchens are the following three: the Plunger, which propels the cork into the bottle where it floats harmlessly out of the way; the Auger, which, with repeated sharp pulls, cuts a narrow opening in the center of the cork through which wine may be gradually dribbled; and the Stripper, a device with two winglike geared levers and a screw which, when it is sunk into the cork, provides the necessary fulcrum so that downward pressure on the handles will remove one or both of them from the mechanism.

Corn-on-the-Cob

Delectable summer vegetable eaten with the hands. Since the sugars in corn begin turning into starch the moment the ears are separated from the stalk, it is often said that one should not pick corn until the cooking water is boiling. Corn-on-the-Cob is a messy dish to eat and one with a lot of unwanted parts to dispose of, such as husks, tassels, silk, and the cobs themselves, and so it's not a bad idea at the same time to warm up the garbage disposal, run a bath or turn on the shower, and get out the dental floss.

Cream

Concentration of fatty substances that forms on the top of unhomogenized milk. Cream is readily obtainable in a variety of forms, including heavy or whipping cream, light cream, half-and-half, clotted cream, sour cream, and crème fraîche. Also available are non-dairy creamers and dessert toppings, which can be purchased at a store or made at home by collecting the fuzz off the back of a refrigerator and blending it over low heat with a mixture of white house paint, liquid soap, fence-post preservative, and hand cream.

Crock

1. Small earthenware soup bowl or storage container often made by earnest counterculture potters in places like Ben-

Corkscrew

Cupboard

nington, Vermont, and Santa Fe, New Mexico. 2. Explanation offered by owner of a store selling such pottery as to why a misshapen bowl with big dollops of gray-green glaze dripping off the edge is a work of art that a cook should be grateful to obtain for $40.

Crudités — Appetizer consisting of raw vegetables like carrots, radishes, scallions, and celery. It is also commonly referred to as crappés, crummés, lousés, or simply bore d'oeuvres.

Crumbs — *1.* Pieces of stale bread, lightly browned and cut into small pieces, used as a coating for fried chicken and in turkey stuffings. 2. Objectionable individuals who offer unsolicited recipes for dishes like fried chicken and roast turkey after taking a bite of yours.

Cupboard — One of a number of places where the gravy boat isn't.

Cutting Board — Any portable knife-resistant surface on which food is cut into pieces that are too large (chopping), too small (dicing), too chunky (cubing), too thin (mincing), or too stringy (shredding) for a given recipe.

D

Diet — The specific types and quantities of food that any given individual will start eating tomorrow, next week, or after the beginning of the new year.

Dining Room — Archaic name for a large, separate room that was once part of the floor plan in American houses and apartments. It is now almost totally replaced by the dining area, the feeding zone, the munching loft, the nutrition nook, the snack foyer, the dinner niche, the culinette, or the repastularium.

Dip *1.* Tasty semiliquid concoction usually served in a small bowl into which one dunks any of a variety of snack foods. *2.* Individual who consumes the entire contents of such a bowl in a quick or greedy fashion.

Dishwasher Extraordinarily convenient kitchen appliance that uses very powerful water jets and high-voltage heating elements to wash, rinse, and dry dishware and cooking utensils. Unfortunately, most dishwashers tend to pulverize delicate china and stemware, and they are not recommended for earthenware, expensive flatware, and some ceramics. Dishwashers vary, of course, but generally they operate using the following basic cleaning cycles: Flood; Soap and Pelt; Wallop; Hammer/Drench; Flush and Pummel; Resoap/Gush/Shred; Joggle and Slosh; Pound and Churn; Rattle/Swish/Thrash/Rinse; and Dry and Weld.

Drawer A mess with a knob on the end.

Dress *1.* To prepare animals such as poultry, game, or fish for cooking by cleaning, skinning, trimming, plucking, or drawing. *2.* To prepare a human for a formal dinner by bathing, shaving, combing, girdling, trussing, exhorting, or threatening.

E

Egg Indispensable cooking ingredient and widely eaten food in its own right, particularly as a breakfast dish and in omelets. Also, in ancient Gallic folk beliefs, one of the six basic elements in the universe, along with butter, flour, cream, wine, and rude waiters.

Drawer

Electric Appliances

Eggnog Traditional Christmas Eve drink made with egg yolks, cream, sugar, nutmeg, and rum or brandy.

Eggnoggin Traditional Christmas morning malaise.

Eggplant Large purple vegetable used in a number of classic dishes, including ratatouille, moussaka, and the celebrated Turkish dish Imam Bayuldi ("The Imam Fainted"). Because eggplant discolors easily and can become bitter, oily, or mushy if improperly cooked, it is also the key ingredient in the less well-known Middle Eastern recipes Imam Krabbiya ("The Imam Grew Petulant"), Imam Barfoosh ("The Imam Threw Up"), and Imam Scimitari ("The Imam Cut Off the Head of the Cook").

Electric Appliances Although some cooks still prefer to do basic tasks by hand, the last two decades have witnessed the introduction of dozens of very welcome electrically powered labor-saving devices that can now be found in millions of kitchens. Of course, there have been a few failures, including: the electric toothpick with gum-o-matic action (1958); the electric paper towel dispenser (1961); the motorized gravy boat (1964); the electrically warmed napkin with decorator cord (1966); the electric serving spoon (1967); and the Green Machine wash 'n' dry salad centrifuge (1969), slightly redesigned and reissued as the Pic 'n' Span portable picnic dishwasher (1971).

English Cooking No one knows for certain the antecedents of the cuisine of the British Isles, but an oft-repeated culinary legend holds that an ancient Saxon shepherd left a lunch of goat cheese in a leather bag in a cool cave, then forgot where he put it. When he came upon it again several weeks later, ravenously hungry, he discovered in the sack a delicate, pungent, perfectly veined piece of Roquefort. Wasting no time, he threw the funny-smelling cheese away, cleaned and boiled the leather bag, and ate it.

English Equivalents

Although America and Britain speak the same language, there are some differences in basic culinary terms that may confuse cooks using British cookbooks or entertaining British dinner guests. Here are a few of the most common:

British	American
Ale	Beer
Cold	Warm
—	Ice
Tea	—
Bun	Biscuit
Biscuit	Cookie, cracker
Crackers	Insane
Interesting	Awful
Very interesting	Horrible
Really very interesting	Dreadful
Peculiar	Inedible
Such a lovely dinner	Jeez, what slop
Toodle-oo	Goodbye
God, I need a drink	God, I need a drink

Entrée

Dinner course that is traditionally served after the whispers and before the groans.

Epicureanism

Ancient Greek philosophy commonly expressed in the phrase "Eat, drink, and be merry." It is but one of countless culinary philosophies, including clean Platonism ("Finish it all, even if it kills you"); à la Cartesianism ("I eat, therefore I am"); and zen Foodism ("What is the sound of one hand signaling for a waiter in a crowded restaurant?").

Epicureanism

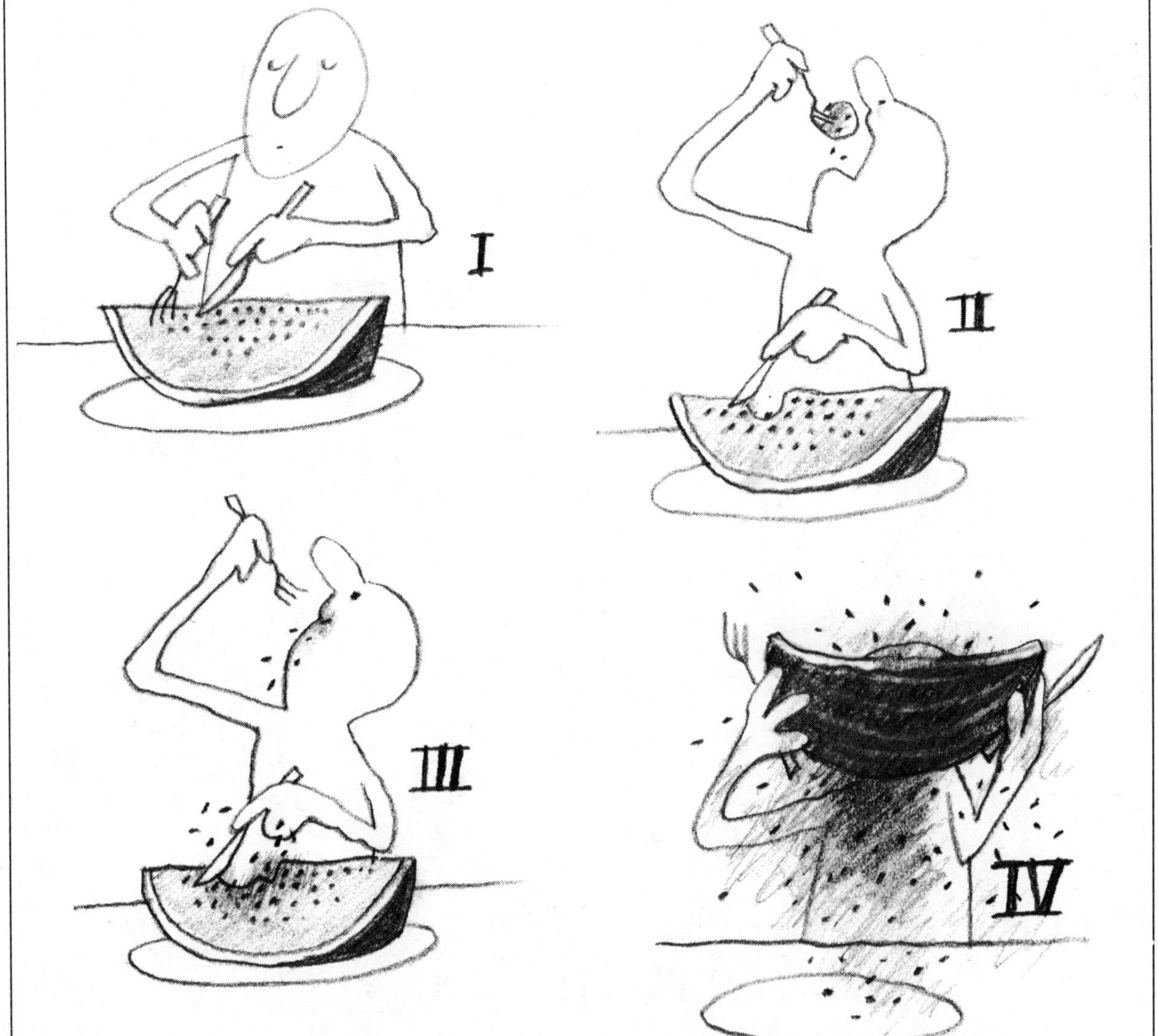

Etiquette

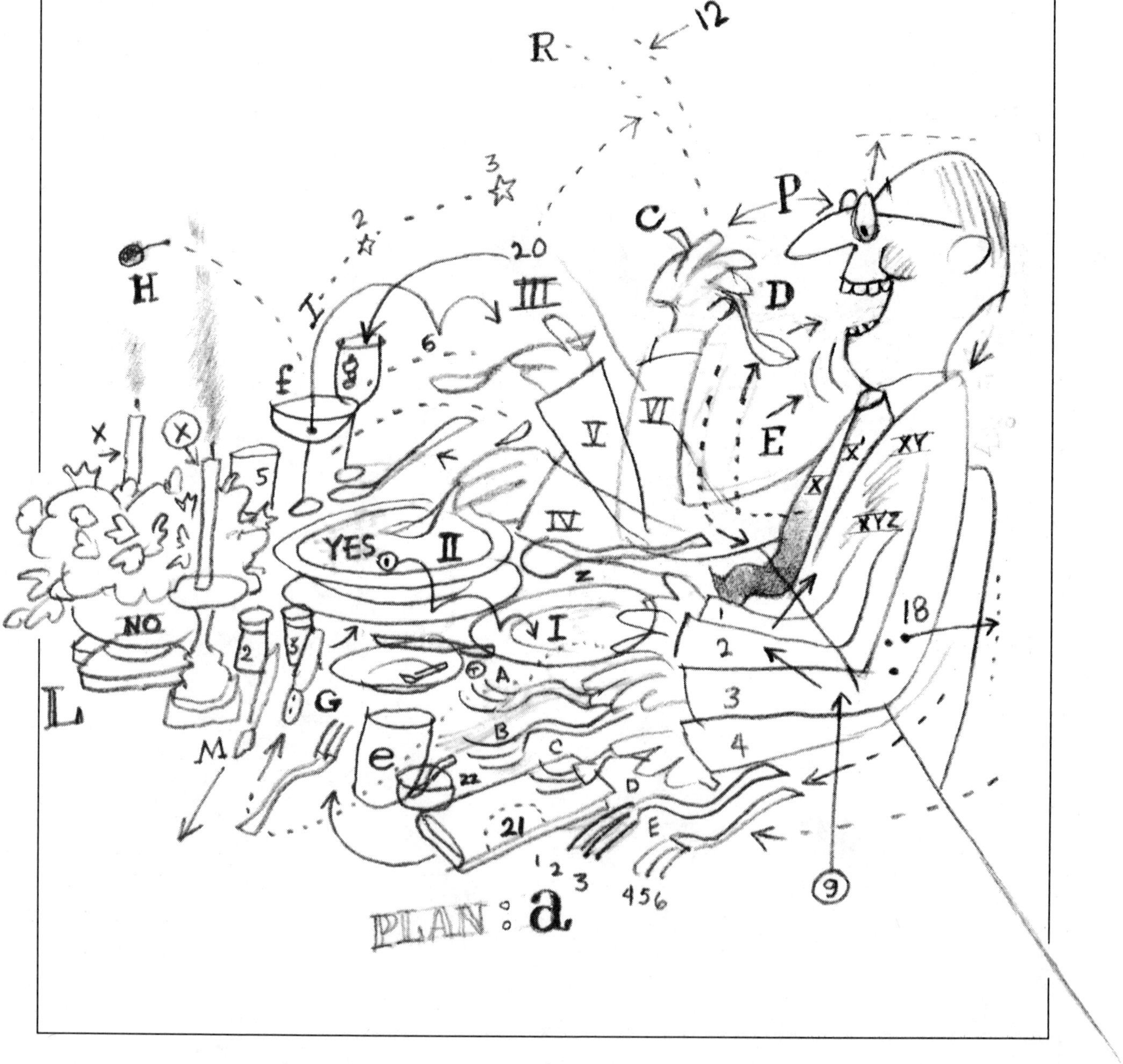

R
12
P
C
D
E
H
2
3
20
III
6
f
g
V
VI
X
XY
XYZ
X
5
IV
YES
II
I
NO
2
3
A
B
C
D
E
G
L
M
e
22
21
18
1
2
3
4
9
1 2 3
456
PLAN: a

Ethnic Cooking Any cuisine typified by strongly flavored dishes which, when prepared by a next-door neighbor, can be enjoyed by everyone living in the immediate vicinity without the necessity of their being invited to dinner.

Etiquette Formal procedure through which you trick the person sitting next to you at a dinner party into eating your salad while you take his or her bread and butter.

F

Fast Food Bland, limited menu, usually consisting of hamburgers, French fries, and milk shakes, served by cooks whose sole culinary skill is the ability to operate a motor vehicle. *See* HEALTH FOOD.

Fats Any of a variety of animal or vegetable products in a solid or semisolid state which, when brought into contact with an article of clothing, leave a blob, smear, or blotch. *See* OILS.

Fermentation Chemical reaction, caused by microbes, that turns malt into belches and grapes into hangovers.

Finger Bowl *1. (n.)* Small dish filled with warm, lemon-scented water in which one bathes the digits after eating food with the hand. *2. (v.)* To propel a radish, melon ball, or Brussels sprout toward another diner's plate.

Fish It is not always easy to tell if fish is truly fresh, rather than frozen and recently thawed, and since tasting a merchant's offerings is obviously impractical one must concentrate on the seller himself. Shake his hand. Is his palm moist and cool to the touch? Is there a telltale ring on his pinkie? Does he have one hand behind his back with the first and second fingers lightly crossed in an unmistakable X? Look him over carefully. Are his eyes bright, shiny, and quick-moving? Are his scales in good operating condition? Does he seem "slimy"? Ask him a question. Does he try to wriggle out of it, or is there perhaps something "fishy" about his patter? When pressed, does he respond firmly or is he slippery? In a word, caveat emptor!

Flan *1.* French custard. *2.* Sound made by French custard hitting a tiled kitchen floor.

Flour The key ingredient in most classic kitchen messes (*hautes messes*), including powdered countertop (*table à la neige*), batter-covered mixing bowls (*bols d'horreur*), and pan with baked-on glop (*pan brûlé grand-merde*).

Food Any plant or animal substance that provides nourishment. There are basically four broad categories of food: carbohydrates, fats, proteins, and individually wrapped chocolates with cherry centers.

Food Additive Any artificial substance added directly or indirectly to a food product. Consumers periodically become agitated about the several thousand chemicals that find their way into processed foods, but industry spokesmen insist on their safety and are frankly at a loss to explain the growing opposition to their use. Some of the most common additives are: abominine, odiose, noxides, detrimenthyl, disgustillates, malevolene, deleteriose, lethalicin, malignite, inauspicene, atrocose, perniciose, appallitol, gum malefic, repugnate, repellate, despicabylic acid, deplorabate, dilapidase, exacerbene, annoylene, dolorose, woebegene, and phobic acid.

SOUP
NUTS

Freezer

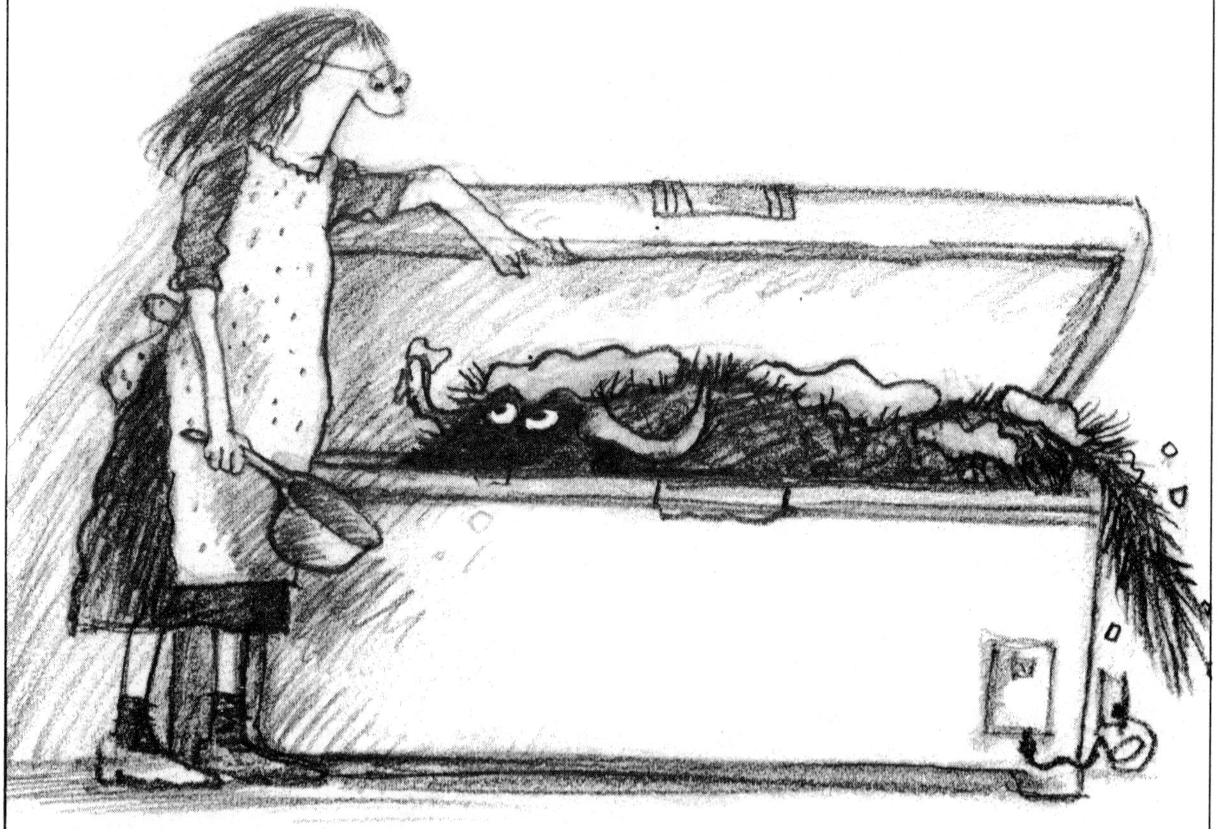

Food Processor

Powerful electric device with very rapidly whirling blades, used for conducting experiments in culinary physics at home, e.g., reducing a bunch of carrots to their basic atomic constituents, the carrotrinos, or subjecting a handful of onions to the conditions that existed at the birth of the universe. The largest food processor in the world today is the Cuisinac, the giant 800,000-volt French machine at Moussy, where scientists have isolated the smallest known food particles, the anti-crouton and the parmeson.

Fork

Basic cooking and eating implement whose appearance on the table in the Middle Ages was preceded by the knife and the spoon, which have been around since prehistoric times in one form or another. The fork has since turned up in countless shapes and adaptations, including the heavy Bowie fork (1828), the rather deadly Italian switch-fork (about 1885), the huge, machete-like Cuban forchete wielded by the cucumberos on the ill-fated zucchini plantations in the Sierra Maestre (1909), and the stiletto-like forchonet mounted on the rifles of the French Culinary Corps in World War I (1914). Persons interested in the fascinating development of this utensil are urged to peruse Felix Borchardt's excellent three-volume work, *The Tines, They Are A'Changin'*.

Freezer

Insulated and refrigerated compartment used to store food for long periods of time without spoiling. The behavior of edible substances at subzero temperatures is quite unpredictable, and, if left untouched in a freezer for a week or more, some foods, such as T-bone steaks, frozen French fries, and pints of ice cream, can inexplicably be transformed into a single two-quart serving of frozen split-pea soup in a large plastic tub.

French Toast

A popular breakfast dish consisting of slices of white bread dipped into a mixture of milk and beaten eggs, fried in butter and served with maple syrup and/or powdered sugar. Variations include: Welsh toast (a slice of white bread fried in a beer batter), Scotch toast (a slice of stale white bread), and Irish toast (beer.)

Frying

Cooking method in which food is immersed in hot oil and quickly browned while the house is slowly smoked.

G

Gadget

Any mechanical device that performs a kitchen task in one-twentieth the time it takes to find it.

Game

A surprisingly large number of people shrink from eating game animals such as duck, rabbit, and deer because in childhood they were exposed to endearing characters like Donald Duck, Peter Rabbit, Bugs Bunny, the Easter Bunny, Thumper, and Bambi. Alas, ingrained habits are difficult to change, but you can protect your children from an inappropriate sentimental aversion to delicious dishes like canard à l'orange, civet de lapin, and venison stew by giving them, as early as possible, some of the illustrated volumes from the excellent *Young Gourmet* series published by the Trencherman Press, including "The Adventures of Fred Duck, Chick Molester," "Roscoe Rabbit and the Gun Bunnies," and "Buck Deer, the Kitten Killer."

Garlic

Aromatic, powerfully flavored herb, added to dishes in amounts ranging from the very heavy (several individual cloves or even an entire head of garlic, mashed or chopped coarsely) to the moderate (a tablespoon or two of diced

NO-WEEP ONION HELMET

JIFFY BANANA SLICER

INDUSTRIAL-STRENGTH JAR OPENER

Gastronomy

garlic or a few shakes of garlic powder) to the very light (one or two sides of Enrico Caruso singing *Cavalleria Rusticana*, played at moderate volume on a small kitchen hi-fi placed not too close to the cooking pot).

Gastronomy The art or science of the preparation and presentation of food. This should not be confused with gastrology, a superstition-laden pseudoscience that purports to predict human destiny based on the fruits and vegetables in season and the number of stars held by the closest restaurant in existence at the time and place of one's birth.

Gazpacho *1.* Tasty, but often quite spicy cold soup made of tomatoes and cucumbers and garnished with croutons, peppers, onions, and scallions. *2.* Nasal sound made by consumer of gazpacho after inhaling a portion of the garnish.

Gelatin A pain in the aspic.

German Food Distinct central European national cookery which, with two notable exceptions, has made a contribution to world cuisine of roughly the same importance as that made by English wines, Swiss seafood dishes, Canadian cheese, and Chinese desserts. *See* HAMBURGER.

Glaze *1.* Confusing cooking term that refers to a number of distinct and complex culinary processes, e.g., to cover with a syrup of egg and sugar; to pass under a flame until brown; to apply an aspic jelly coating; or to coat with a white sauce. *2.* Distant, unfocused look that comes into the eye of a cook after confronting a recipe that calls for a food to be glazed.

Gorgonzola *1.* Delicious, creamy, powerfully flavored Italian blue cheese. *2.* Large, gooey movie monster featured in a series of Italian science-fiction films of the early 1960s, including

Gorgonzola gli Stupendi (Mighty Gorgonzola), Gorgonzola Frappara il Autostrada (Gorgonzola Hits the Road), Gorgonzola e la Lutta (Gorgonzola Goes on Strike), Gorgonzola e gli Rossi (Gorgonzola Joins the Communist Party), and *Ciao, Gorgonzola! (A Monster and a Woman).*

Gourmand	Serious eater whose culinary opinions carry at least as much weight as he does.
Gourmet	Anyone who, when you fail to finish something strange or revolting, remarks that it's an acquired taste and that you're leaving the best part.
Gourmet Frozen Food	Major innovation in the convenience food industry that allows consumers to enjoy airline meals at home.
Gravy	*See* TIE.
Grocery Bag	Large brown paper sack in which purchases of food and kitchen products are transported from the market prior to being distributed along the path to the front of the house, the landing outside an apartment, or the stairs leading to the back door.
Grocery Store Cart	Self-propelled wire-mesh food carrier with three functioning wheels and a handle with mayonnaise on it.
Grocery Store Clerk	Employee of a food store or supermarket who packs a grocery bag with, typically, a sack of potato chips, two light bulbs, a dozen eggs, a container of yogurt, a bottle of apple juice, and a melon, in that order.
Grouse	*1. (n.)* Tasty game bird found in countries throughout the Northern Hemisphere. *2. (v.)* To complain audibly after encountering a mouthful of buckshot in one's grouse or, alternatively, finding a Frank Perdue Rock Cornish game hen tag tied to its foot.

Gourmet Frozen Food

Health Food

H

Ham The upper part of the hind leg of a hog, usually cured and/or smoked. There are two basic types of American ham: the handmade country hams like the Smithfield, which is salted, smoked for a week or more, and then aged for as long as two years in special warehouses; and the mass-produced urban hams like the Richmond, which is given a coating of highway salt, blasted with diesel exhaust for 30 seconds, then left in a bus station locker for a week.

Hamburger It's an odd fact that the two most quintessentially American foods—the hamburger and the frankfurter—derive their names and presumably their origins from a pair of German cities not particularly noted for their cuisines. What makes the happy appearance of these universally loved comestibles in the United States even more remarkable is that the culinary milieu from which they emerged was so unpromising, and Americans should be very thankful that early German immigrants to their country brought with them the hamburger and the frankfurter and not the Augsburger (meat pie stuffed with ground ox hearts and kale), the Würzburger (cooked liver smothered in shaved turnips and served on a prune strudel), the Magdeburger (whole beef tongue on a celery seed roll), the Schweinfurter (goat sausage and lard on a dumpling), or the Erfurter (pig's foot in a potato skin topped with cold noodles).

Health Food Any food whose flavor is indistinguishable from that of the package in which it is sold. *See* JUNK FOOD.

Helpful Guest Well-intentioned individual who assists in the process of converting the good china into the everyday china.

Herbs and Spices Basic flavoring substances consisting of the leaves (in the case of herbs) and seeds (in the case of spices) of various aromatic plants, intended to be used in very small amounts and typically added to a dish when the cook first mixes the ingredients; once again while he stirs the pot during a distracting telephone call; and one more time immediately following his second martini.

Hollandaise Complex egg-based sauce usually consisting of two or three minor miscalculations combined with at least one major mistake.

Honey Sugary liquid substance produced by bees from the nectar of flowers and used as a spread or sweetener. Incidentally, a full jar of honey dropped onto a kitchen floor was recently voted Mess of the Year by the readers of *Modern Annoyance Magazine*, narrowly edging out a slow puncture leak in the bottom of a family-size plastic cola bottle stored on the top shelf of a refrigerator and a 10-pound flour sack with a torn bottom placed in the back of a cupboard.

I

Ice Cream Enormously popular chilled dessert dish made from cream, eggs, sugar, and flavorings. Despite the appearance of hundreds of exotic varieties, the old standbys—chocolate, vanilla, strawberry, and coffee—are perennial favorites according to industry sources. However, the least liked flavors do change. Last year, they were, in descending order of disapproval: Danish Prune, Margarine Walnut, Pumpkin Marshmallow Chunk, Cinnamelon, Cranapricot, Persimmon Mint, and Manila Flap.

Herbs and Spices

Junk Food

Imported Packed in a box, can, carton, or bottle with a label containing lies in a foreign language.

Insinkerator Mechanical food-disposal unit based on the principle of the teenager.

Instant Food Any food that can be prepared in less time than it takes to taste the result, throw it away, and clean up the pot. *See* JUNK FOOD.

J

Jams and Jellies Sweet fruit confections served at breakfast with toast, muffins, or other baked goods. Oddly enough, jams and jellies are considered diet foods, since the calories expended in opening the jars and packets in which they are sold greatly exceeds the number consumed in the course of eating their contents.

Jeroboam Double-magnum container of wine, equal in contents to four regular-size bottles. Wine also comes in bottle sizes called Rehoboam (6), Methuselah (8), Salmanazar (12), Balthazar (16), and Nebuchadnezzar (24). Quite recently, due to the influence of airlines on the wine industry, it has become available in the following miniature sizes: Ebeneezer (8 oz.), Silasmarner (6 oz.), Curmudgeon (4 oz.), Nibelungen (2 oz.), Leprechaun (1 oz.), Amoeboam (½ oz.), and Paramecium (¼ oz.)

Junk Food Any packaged processed food such as cookies, candy, and potato chips, the bulk of whose nutritional value is contained in the box or bag it comes in. *See* NATURAL FOOD.

Junket

Proper name of the once widely prepared infant's dish, composed of the solids (curds) and liquids (whey) in coagulated milk, that Miss Muffet was eating in the old Mother Goose nursery rhyme. Both the rhyme and the foodstuff have been updated in the latest edition of the beloved Ms. *Goose's Nonsexist Developmental Verses*:

A woman named Muffet, a mayor,
sat in a large swivel chair
eating tofu after a refreshing jog.

A member of the insect-American race
invaded her personal space
and she engaged it in meaningful dialogue.

K

Kettle

Container used to bring water for coffee or tea to a boil. Some kettles emit a pleasant whistling sound or tone when the water begins to boil, but even the simplest ones automatically signal that all the water has been transformed into steam by gradually turning black and emitting a sharp, metallic odor.

Kitchen

Large room with rugged, easy-to-maintain surfaces designed to permit pots, pans, crockery, and other cooking utensils to be thrown at spouses, offspring, relatives, or guests without causing impossible clean-up problems or lasting damage.

Kitchen Cabinet

Storage area containing items that should have been put somewhere else.

Kettle

Knife

Kiwi

Insipid, but nutritious lemon-size fruit from New Zealand that became a major fad food after its vivid green flesh made it a mainstay of nouvelle cuisine. Despite its growing acceptance, it is hardly likely ever to surpass traditional fruits like the apple in popularity, though kiwi-bobbing was reported at a New York disco last Halloween, the fuzzy fruit is given to favored teachers at progressive schools on the eastern seaboard, and in California they say that a kiwi a day keeps the acupuncturist away.

Knife

The basic kitchen cutting tool. There are several different sizes, each designed for a particular task, and various metal alloys to choose from, but regardless of which type one buys it is essential to "break in" or "season" the new knife immediately after purchase because, frankly, most chefs become too attached to these handsome tools and the inevitable misuse of a favorite one by others causes unnecessary friction. To accomplish this process of preparation, first hold the handle over an open flame, burning it in one or two places. Then strike the blade several times on the sharpened side against a brick or cinderblock until there are deep nicks in the cutting edge. Next, hold the knife by the end of the handle over a cement garage floor or stone patio and drop it repeatedly until the point breaks off. And finally, leave the knife in the sink under a dripping faucet until blotches of discoloration appear. You may now put it in a drawer, confident that the next time you go to use it, it will be in the same condition you left it in.

Kohlrabi

Curious vegetable sometimes called the cabbage turnip, since it consists of a turnip-like stem and thick, cabbagey leaves. Both parts are edible, but most sensible cooks cut off and discard the leaves, then throw away the stem.

L

Ladle The only thing that is edible in a pot of leek soup.

Lamb Delicate, flavorful meat that has never gained much popularity in America, since by tradition it is invariably grossly overcooked. Typical recipes include Wallet of Lamb with Hot Wet Sauce, Gray Roast in Its Own Sludge, Sliced Blunt Instrument, and Unknown Meatlike Substance with Green Toothpaste Jelly.

Lemon Tart, tangy citrus fruit much used in cooking. For some reason, lemons always contain exactly twice or precisely two-thirds the amount of lemon juice called for in any given recipe.

Lentil *1.* Bland seed of a leguminous plant similar to a vetch, used in soups and stews. 2. Yiddish word for a dinner guest who comes into the kitchen, takes lids off pots, stirs the contents, adds seasonings, and then complains bitterly about the result.

Lettuce Term that properly refers to plants of the genus *Lactuca* commonly used in salads—among them, Bibb and Boston, oak leaf, ruby, and romaine lettuce and mâche—but is often used erroneously to include other salad greens like arugula, escarole, and raddiccio. In the last year for which figures were available, Americans bought 19.7 pounds of lettuce and salad greens per person, of which they ate 6.1 pounds, moved 4.6 pounds around their plates with a fork, pretended to find a bug on 2.3 pounds, slipped .9 pound into houseplant pots, and courteously left a generous 5.8 pounds in the salad bowl for others to enjoy.

Lobster

Everyone loves these delectable crustaceans, but many cooks are squeamish about placing them into boiling water alive, which is the only proper method of preparing them. Frankly, the easiest way to eliminate your guilt is to establish theirs by putting them on trial before they're cooked. The fact is, lobsters are among the most ferocious predators on the sea floor, and you're helping reduce crime in the reefs. Grasp the lobster behind the head, look it right in its unmistakably guilty eyestalks and say, "Where were you on the night of the 21st?", then flourish a picture of a scallop or a sole and shout, "Perhaps this will refresh that crude neural apparatus you call a memory!" The lobster will squirm noticeably. It may even take a swipe at you with one of its claws. Incorrigible. Pop it into the pot. Justice has been served, and shortly you and your guests will be, too.

M

Macadamia

The only well-known Australian nut that hasn't raced yachts or served as prime minister.

Macaroni and Cheese

Simple-to-prepare, classic casserole dish that was once a commonplace of dinner parties and "socials." Alas, the revolution in food tastes has made such humble concoctions unwelcome to those with sophisticated palates, but if this recipe is one of your favorites, you can still serve it under the name Maccheroni con Formaggio Velveeta di Amerigo Vespucci. Be careful to present it in an earthenware casserole, and if there are any leftovers, don't say, "Well, guess I'll just shoot this stuff into the old dog dish"; say, "Excuse me while I transfer these *oddzi* and *enzi* into the *dischetta della poochini.*"

Lobster

Margarine Vile butter substitute invented, incredibly, by a French chemist who was tried for his crime at the Court Bouillon, the noted culinary tribunal in Paris, and sentenced to a long prison term on Devil's Island. While there, the incorrigible miscreant managed, using borrowed and stolen materials, to devise a method of preserving and mass-producing mayonnaise and to concoct the world's first non-dairy creamer.

Marinade Any flavored liquid mixture in which a dish whose recipe you just looked up after deciding to serve it this evening should have been soaking since at least last night.

Meal Assortment of hard-to-avoid, potentially filling foodstuffs that precede dessert.

Meat Basically speaking, any food that is easy to prepare, has a delicious flavor, costs too much, is bad for you, and wouldn't taste better with ice cream on it.

Meat Loaf Pâté produced by an excessively honest or totally unimaginative cook.

Metric Measurements The exclusive use of the metric system in all the significant culinary countries of Europe and its gradual introduction into cookbooks in America require the home chef to have some familiarity with the basic metric terms and equivalents. What follows is a brief listing of the most important:

1 KILOSMIDGEN = 100 millidashes
1 DECADOLLOP = 10 centipinches
1 HECTODRIB = 1,000 microdabs
1 DECISOUPÇON = 10 hectahints
10 CENTIJIGGERS = 1 kilosnort

Meat

Microwave Oven

Microwave Oven Space-age kitchen appliance that uses the principle of radar to locate and immediately destroy any foods placed within its cooking compartment.

Milk Basic dairy product. There are various kinds of milk, including skimmed, evaporated, and condensed, but the form in which it is usually encountered by cooks, particularly in households with a large number of children, is vanished, depleted, or consumed, typically consisting of a quarter-inch of slightly sour white liquid in the bottom of a one-gallon carton.

Mondae A vanilla ice-cream soda made with Alka-Seltzer.

Mrs. Beeton Legendary English author of the classic *Book of Household Management* (1861). Though somewhat quaintly written, much of her work has application today, with the possible exception of the chapters on the proper method of disciplining servants ("One should beat lightly with a short leather strap until an attitude of contrition is produced, but not so long as to produce an excess of tears, which spoil the effect, or worse still, to cause the giving of notice which occasions the bother of obtaining on short notice a suitable replacement"); the aging of tradesmen's bills ("Statements of purchases on account should be put in a dark place for at least six months to prevent their senders from becoming familiar or friendly in the American manner"); and the feeding of children ("The provision of food to children should perforce be as much a source of education as of nutrition, and thus I recommend that they be fed foods each month beginning with a successive letter of the alphabet, such as Apples, Bannock, Chowder, and Dumplings, and concluding, if sources of supply may be found, with Yams and Zucchini").

Mushrooms Delightfully flavored fungi that are much used in cooking. Europeans are avid harvesters of wild mushrooms, but Americans are generally deterred by the possibility of accidentally plucking one of the poisonous varieties like *Amanita muscaria*, the dread "death cap." This is a pity since there is nothing like the taste of fresh wild mushrooms, especially morels, cepes or red caps, chanterelles, hens of the woods, and some of the puffballs, and, for that matter, the lethal types have their uses, too, particularly in the hands of a gifted cook who knows how to exploit the problem-solving potential of the kitchen by serving such delicacies as *Nemesis materlegalis* ("mother-in-law's blight"), *Dux eradicans* ("bosses' bane"), *Infidelis maledicti* ("cheater's curse"), and *Publicanus toxicanus* ("taxman's torment").

N

Napkin Cloth or paper hand towel which, in formal entertaining, is put on the wrong side of the plate under the knife that is only right for fish or in a water goblet placed where the other kind of wineglass should have gone.

Natural Food Any processed food characterized by the removal of a few injurious additives from the contents and the addition of a large number of spurious adjectives on the package.

Noodles Honestly. Nobody, but nobody, calls them noodles anymore. Wash your mouth out with kir and *see* PASTA.

Nouvelle Cuisine A child's portion served to an adult.

Nutritional Information A series of reasons you don't believe for not eating food you like given by people you wouldn't want to have dinner with.

Napkin (The Buffet)

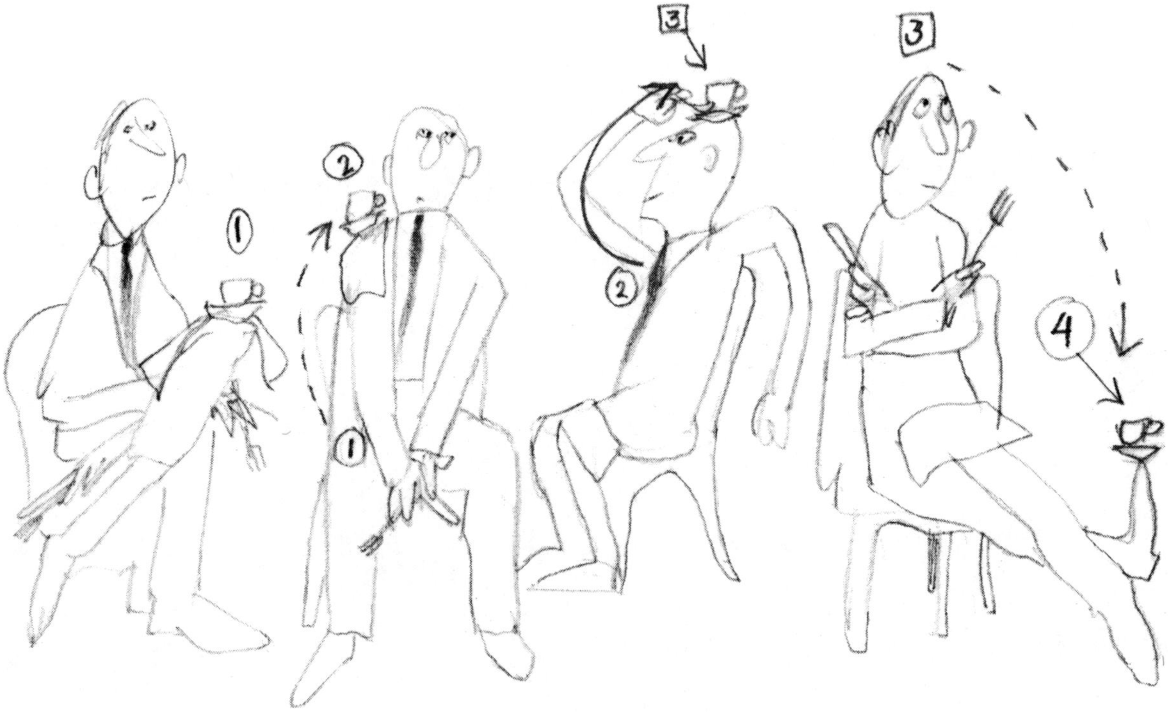

Oven

O

Oils	Any of a variety of cooking substances in a liquid state which, when brought into contact with an article of clothing, leave a stain, spot, or smudge. *See* FATS.
Onion	The only foodstuff that causes tears prior to being cooked or served.
Orange	Although many people eat varieties of this flavorful citrus fruit in halves or sections, the vast majority of the American crop is converted into juice either at home, where oranges are squeezed to yield the delectable fresh breakfast treat, or in processing plants, where the fruit is converted into a number of commodities that are marketed under the following descriptive names mandated by the FTC to specify the amount of actual orange juice each contains: orange juice, frozen orange concentrate, orange-type beverage, orange-flavored drink, orange-colored mixture, orange-like compound, orange-type product, yellow substance, coffee shop liquid, and airline fluid.
Outdoor Grill	Portable barbecuing stove designed to cook meats over a fire of charcoal briquettes. The chief characteristics of this type of fuel are that it will not light in the presence of wind or the absence of a quart of explosive petroleum or paraffin starter; it emits smoke and noxious fumes only in the direction of individuals standing nearby; and it invariably reaches its peak heating temperature 30 minutes before or 90 minutes after food is placed over it.
Oven	Compact home incinerator used for the disposing of bulky pieces of meat and poultry.

Oven Mitt A partially charred grease stain that fits over the hand.

Oyster Sweet, delicately flavored shellfish. Probably the most famous oyster recipe is Oysters Rockefeller, a dish said to have been concocted at Antoine's in New Orleans for the legendary multimillionaire and commonly thought to consist of oysters cooked with bread crumbs, scallions, spices, and butter. In fact, the original recipe was invented by John D. Rockefeller himself, and is far simpler:

- Obtain 6,000 prime oysters.
- Have the servants open the darn things and cut up about 20 dozen lemons. (Count knives afterwards.)
- Get what's-his-name to ring up the usual crowd and tell them to hoof it over to the mansion pronto.
- Chill 5 cases of the best Dom Pérignon, and 50 of that slightly off Bollinger for when they get squiffy.
- Arrange with Reverend Whoosis to have the shells trucked to the needy for mattress stuffing or for Xmas presents if it's the holiday season.

P

Pancake A flat cake made of batter and cooked in a pan or on a griddle. There is some evidence, according to food historians, that the pancake (in this case, a simple water-and-meal confection) was the first prepared food, and in fact, in the ruins of an ancient (3200 B.C.) village in Crete fortuitously preserved by volcanic ash, an underground kitchen was unearthed which contained a bronze pan, a crude iron spatula, a leather apron with the inscription "Look on in awe, mortals—a demigod is at work," and, stuck on the ceiling, the fossilized remains of 71 pancakes.

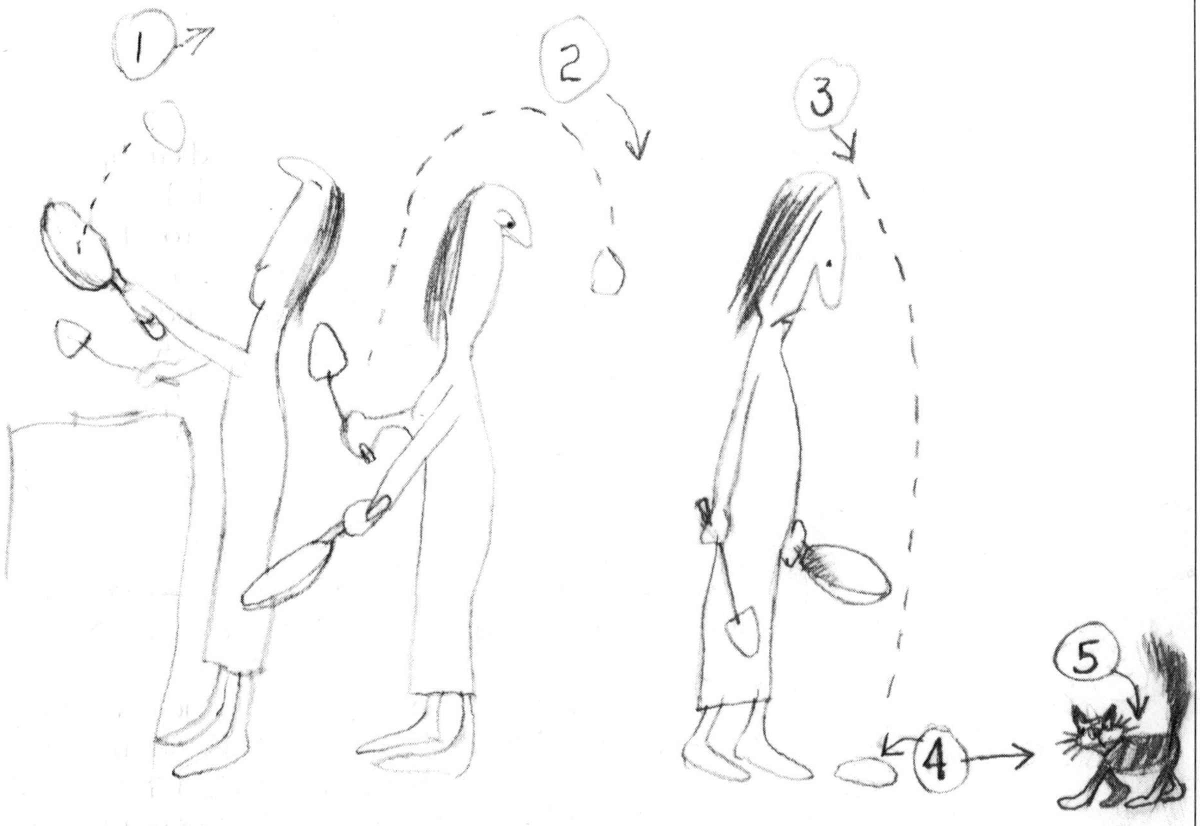

1
2
3
4
5

Pasta

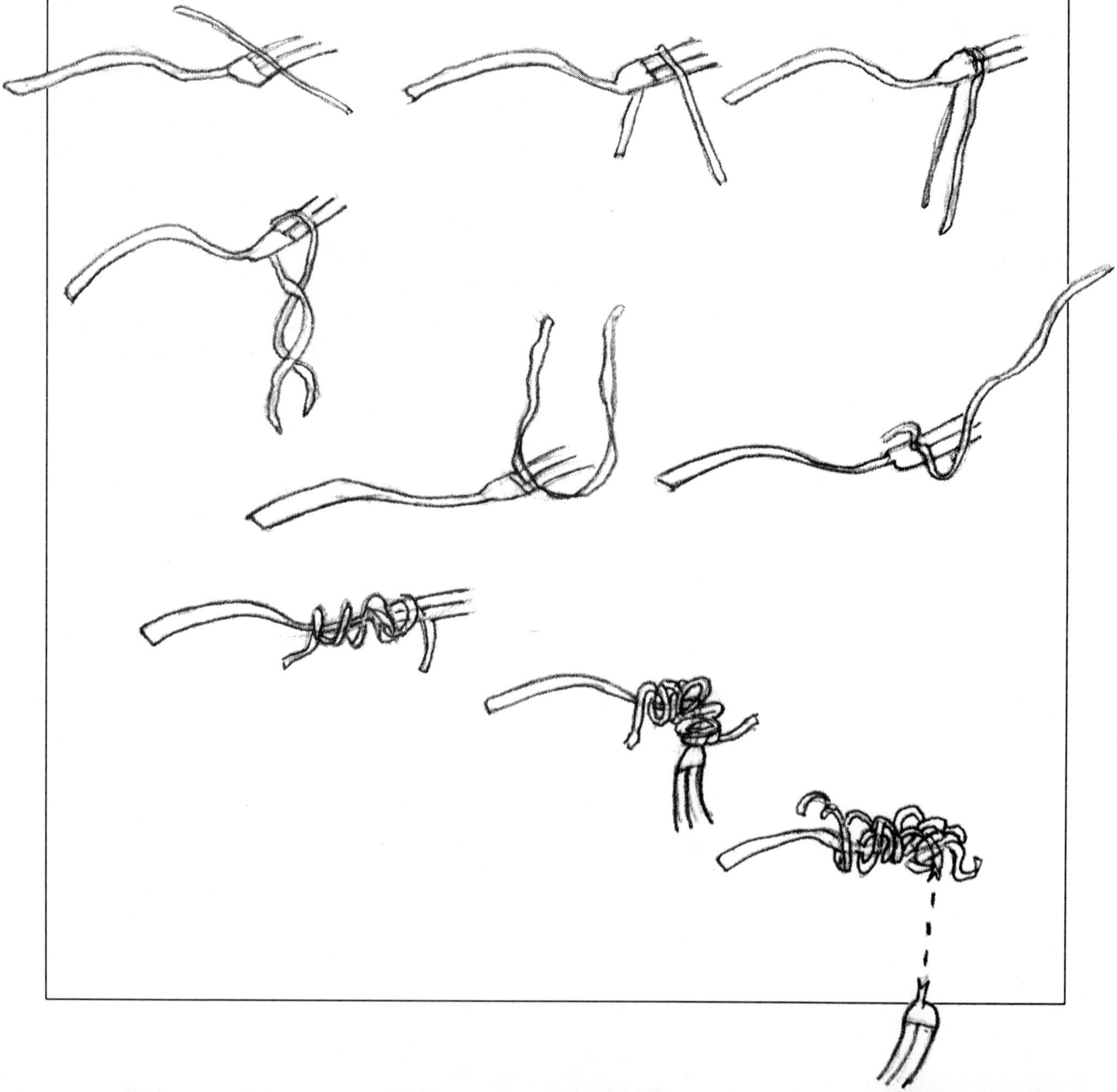

Pasta

A mixture of semolina flour, water, and sometimes egg, extruded through perforated cylinders to produce an almost endless variety of shapes. Pasta, both fresh and dried, has become very popular in recent years, and the more familiar types—spaghetti, cannelloni, linguine, ravioli, tortellini, and gnocchi, to name a few—are the basis for a host of delicious, easily made Italian dishes. There are, however, at least 500 different kinds of pasta, and to give a sense of the incredible diversity of fanciful shapes that exist, here is a short sampling of some of the lesser known types: Gucchi (tiny handbags, stuffed with cheese); Fellini (uneven lengths of noodles with minute sprocket holes, cut at random); Pirelli (little flat tires); Alitalietta (miniature airplanes, filled with garlic); Telefoni (a tangle of long, wire-thin spaghetti); Picopocatelli (pinched purses of pasta, filled with various things); and Autostradolini (a mixture of Fiatti, Ferrari, and Lamborghine, all mashed together).

Peas

When fresh, peas are among the tastiest of all vegetables, although they are notoriously difficult to eat. In fact, the ability to eat 100 peas with no more than four passes of the fork is one of the exacting tests in the grueling training of the French army's Toques Rouges, the elite paratroopers of the crack Batterie de Cuisine whose mission it is to penetrate enemy territory in time of war to sample restaurants and determine which ones are to be spared. Among the other skills that must be perfected are: removing the cork from a wine bottle in absolute silence with the bare hands; securing a table in a completely full restaurant in five minutes flat without killing the maître d' or impersonating the president of the Republic; filleting a turbot with a nail file; mastering hand-to-hand combat with a stale baguette; and eating an artichoke while handcuffed.

Peaches and Pears Succulent fruits that come in two basic types: those customarily grown by gardeners and bred for their juiciness and flavor, and the commercial kinds selected for their amenability to mechanical harvest. In the case of peaches, the garden varieties are the freestone and the clingstone, while those encountered in the market are the curbstone, the pavingstone, and the allstone. Common garden pears are the Anjou, Comice, Bartlett, Bosc, and Seckel; those found in the produce section are the Doorknob, Sashweight, Ballpeen, Pumice, and Sandbag.

Picnic Any meal eaten more than 100 yards from the nearest bathroom.

Pineapple Juicy and flavorful tropical fruit. Pineapples will not ripen after being harvested and are quite perishable when picked ripe. Hence, to be really fresh, they must be shipped by jet from their main source, Hawaii, and the great variation in the quality of pineapples on the market is due to the fact that they can easily become sour and acidic if their flight was bumpy, if they were seated next to a bunch of bananas the whole time, if they had to change planes in Cincinnati, or if the movie was something awful like *The Big Chunk* or *The Blender of Doom*.

Pizza Wonderful Neapolitan culinary invention consisting of cheese, tomatoes, and other ingredients and flavorings on a crisp pie crust. It can be obtained completely cooked and packed in a flat cardboard takeout package at many pizzerias, but a word of warning: although it is both appropriate and thoughtful to bring a neatly boxed pastry, cake, or dessert pie to a dinner party, it is generally considered rude to bring a pizza.

Pineapple (Spotting Ripeness by Eye)

Pork

Pork The meat of pigs, which is available in such forms as roasts and chops, bacon, ham, pork sausage, salt pork, spare ribs, and cracklings. These foods, properly prepared, are absolutely delectable, and so it is unfortunate indeed that their consumption is prohibited to strict adherents of several religions. Equally unfortunate is the fact that for those individuals who, in this time of widespread questioning of traditional religious beliefs, may be seeking some new form of spiritual discipline, there is no known denomination that forbids the eating of spinach, liver, lima beans, coleslaw, fruit cocktails, canned peas, pot roast, or rhubarb.

Porridge Thick oatmeal rarely found on American breakfast tables since children were granted limited standing in federal courts to sue their parents. The name is an amalgamation of the words "*p*utrid," "h*orr*id" and "slu*dge*."

Potato Flavorful tuber that is an important element in western cuisine. Nutritionists dismiss potatoes as low-value foodstuffs despite their clear classification as vegetables, but the fact is that they contain large amounts of potatium, spudine, and tateryl, and, depending on how they are prepared, mashanese, chipicin, snacktic acid, fryaline, bakein, lyonnase, dauphinose, duchessein, gratine, and rissolein.

Pots and Pans An assortment of variously shaped dents, scorch marks, rust spots, tarnishes, and chips with loose handles and missing lids.

Preheat To turn on the heat in an oven for a period of time before cooking a dish so that the fingers may be burnt when the food is put in as well as when it is taken out.

Preservative Any addition to an edible product that increases the life of the food while shortening the life of the consumer.

Q

Quahog

Large, hard-shelled mollusk used in the preparation of clam chowder. The name is derived from the word *poquahock*, translated roughly as "a dollar with a snack inside," in the language of the Narragansett Indians of Rhode Island who, like other native American tribes, used the shells as money, or wampum. Today, clams cost a clam apiece in many restaurants, the shells are used for ashtrays, the Narragansetts are a beer, and Rhode Island is best known for chicken. There is probably a moral in this somewhere.

Quail

1. (n.) Small bird in the partridge family, known familiarly as the bobwhite from its characteristic call and considered a great delicacy by lovers of game. *2. (v.)* To recoil in horror at the sight of a pair of recently deceased songbirds nestled on one's plate.

R

Range

Multipurpose kitchen appliance that cooks food by employing one of two basic heating principles: gas leak or short circuit. Ranges typically consist of a stove top with one, three or five functioning burners and two separate cooking compartments: one for baking, with a door that will not close, and one for broiling, with a door that will not open. The intensity and length of heating in these ovens are controlled by dials that indicate the temperature inside to the nearest 100° and a clock that displays the exact time in Madagascar.

Quail

Recipe

Recipe A series of step-by-step instructions for preparing ingredients you forgot to buy in utensils you don't own to make a dish the dog won't eat the rest of.

Refrigerator Mechanically refrigerated storage compartment that is carefully calibrated to maintain a temperature low enough to lightly freeze salad greens stored in a lower vegetable drawer yet high enough to permit a gallon of milk placed on the upper shelf to spoil.

Restaurant Where the remaining courses of a meal that began with a flambéed appetizer in a home dining room are served.

Rhubarb *1.* Foul-tasting leafy plant whose sweetened, stewed stems are made into pies or served in a dish as a sort of pudding. *2.* A squabble or quarrel such as might erupt after someone is served a vegetable for dessert.

Rice Tropical and subtropical cereal grain that is widely eaten throughout the world but is not a very significant factor in the American diet. The proper cooking of rice is generally conceded to be an art, but various cooking authorities agree on nothing else: some say adding salt to rice ruins it, others say its absence makes the rice tasteless; some insist on putting a little butter in with the rice to keep the grains separate, others protest that this just makes them greasy; some claim the cooking should be begun in hot water and the rice later rinsed in cold, others take exactly the opposite position; most argue that rice should be simmered in a tightly closed pot, but there are those who contend with equal fervor that it should be boiled uncovered in a large volume of water; and though a majority dismiss instant rice as a flavorless abomination, a vocal few assert that it is both tasty and convenient. Perhaps because of this innate capac-

Sandwich (Variations on a Classic)

Bagel, lox and tofu.

Bananas, leeks and trout.

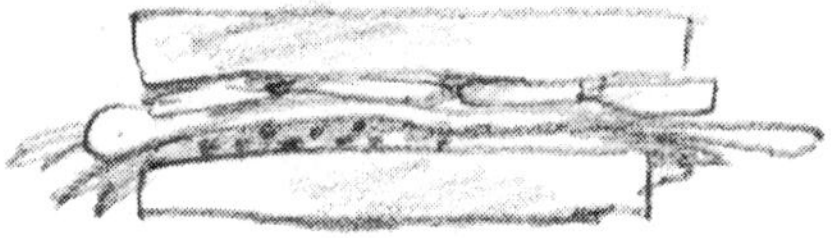

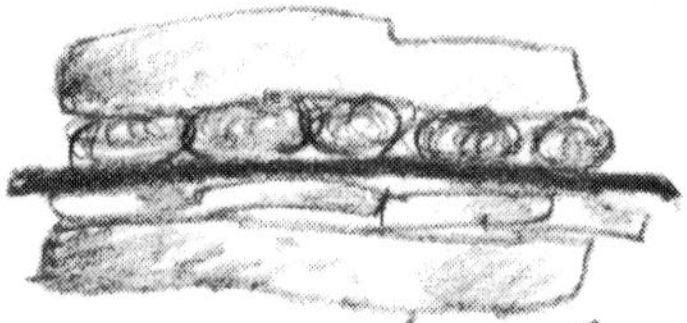

Brussels sprouts, licorice and turnips.

Bologna, limas and truffles.

Broccoli, liver and tuna.

ity to inspire contention, rice is traditionally flung at the newly married as an apt symbol of the many years of fatheaded wrangling, pointless argument, and tiresome discourse lying ahead of the happy couple.

Roasting The process of cooking a large piece of meat or a fowl in an oven. The two basic roasting methods, high-temperature and low-temperature, produce few differences in flavor or appearance of the meat or fowl, and hence the choice really comes down to whether the cook wishes the roast to be done two and a half hours before guests arrive or four hours after they depart.

S

Sale Item Any supermarket item that, for a given period of time, costs half of twice what it should.

Sandwich Credit for the invention of this classic lunch item composed of a meat or other filling between two slices of bread is correctly given to its namesake, John Montagu, fourth Earl of Sandwich (1718–1792), who, as the story goes, wanted a meal that could be eaten without interrupting his gambling, for which he had a passion. But his equally creative betting companions from throughout the royal houses of Europe were apparently inspired by his burst of culinary genius to contribute their own refinements, and they deserve mention here as well: Prince Luigi Pastrami; Graf von Pumpernickel; the Marquise de Mayonnaise; Vidkund Gustaf Smorgasbord; Jean Buffet, Vicomte de Casserole; Don Antonio Saladbar; and Archduke Bakonyi of Lettusky-Tomatoff.

Sardines One of the eight items most commonly found in kitchen cupboards at 2 A.M. in the place where the peanut butter used to be. The others are translucent Chinese noodles, sesame seeds, millet, a jar of cocktail onions, a block of bitter baking chocolate, a can of white clam sauce, and a box of flavored toothpicks.

Sauces There are, in French cuisine alone, at least 200 sauces, but they are all members of two broad categories: the white sauces, like Allemande, Béarnaise, Béchamel, Printanière, Ravigote, and Soubise; and the brown sauces, such as Bigarade, Bordelaise, Bourguignonne, Châteaubriand, and Périgourdine. In home cooking there is a third major category, the black sauces, which includes Burnaise, Châteaufumé, Messaline, Napalmel, Pyrotechnière, Vésuvienne, Mondieu, and Sacrébleu.

Sausage *1.* Various parts of pigs and cows, such as pieces of, well, sort of odds and ends, stuffed into lengths of, you know, those things from down inside there somewhere. *2.* Ooogh.

Sauté Classic French cooking technique in which foods are pan-fried quite quickly in very hot oil. To sauté foods properly, a cook must have a large, heavy, flat-sided copper skillet; a pencil-thin mustache; a small French motorcar, preferably a Citroën; a seven-eighths-smoked unfiltered Gauloise cigarette held loosely in the lower lip; an exact knowledge of the location and function of the liver; a prominently displayed medal for some exceptional service to the Republic during the war, such as deliberately teaching German soldiers the wrong endings to irregular verbs; and bizarre political beliefs centering on some novel governmental concept such as imprisoning all cats or giving cheese the vote.

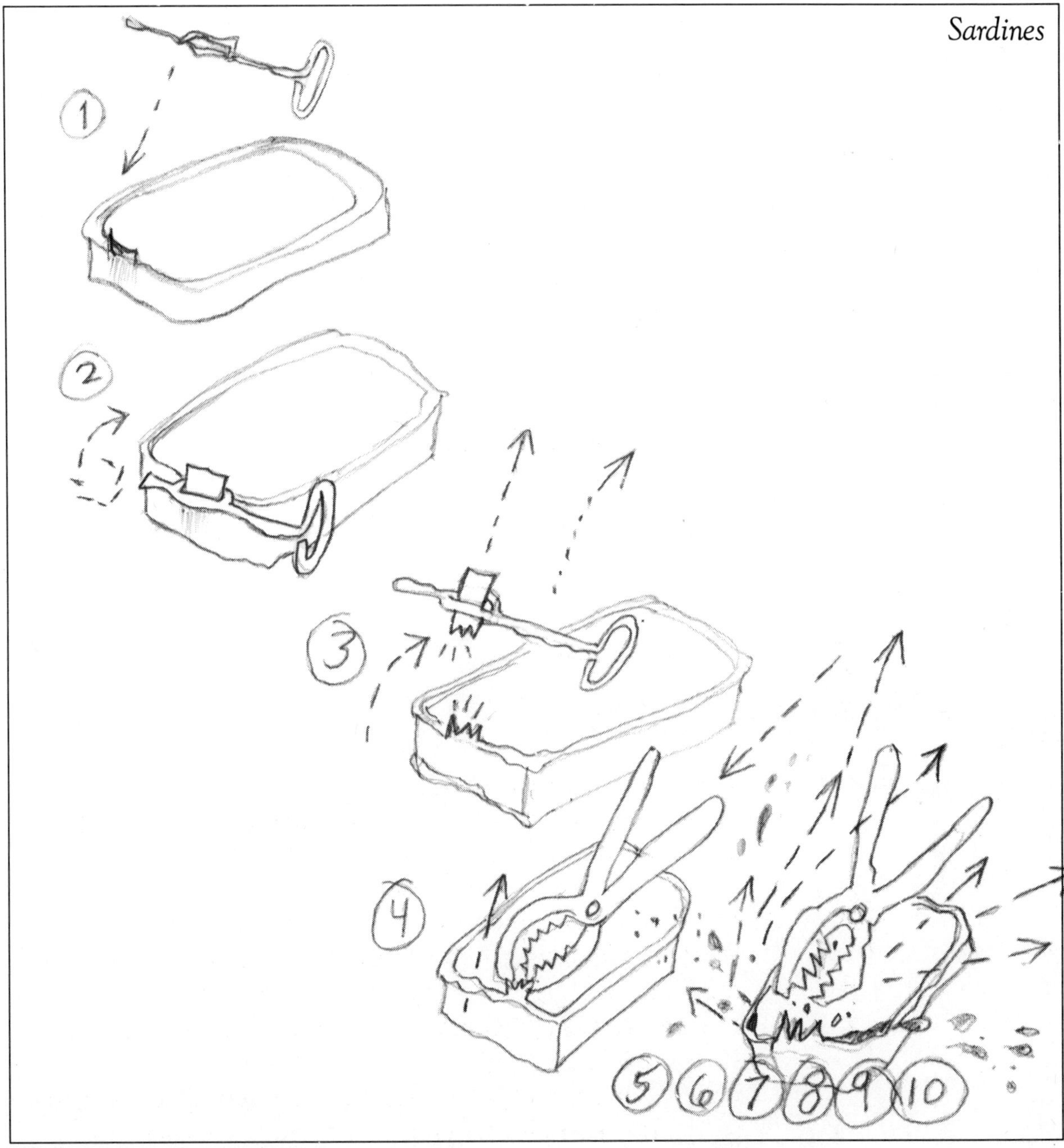

Sardines

Silver

Scales	Unpleasant, troublesome things encountered on fish and on bathroom floors.
Shears	Large, indispensable kitchen scissors found in tool kits, sewing baskets, tackle boxes, and toy chests.
Shelf Life	The amount of time a given product can remain on display in a supermarket. This is customarily defined as (*a*) the period before it explodes, melts, turns a funny color, emits a noticeable odor, or begins to interest antique dealers; (*b*) a period of time prior to the point where the English language has changed sufficiently to make its name or the description of its contents meaningless; or (*c*) that period of time during which the first two digits of the year of its manufacture correspond to those of the century in which it is being offered for sale.
Silver	Eye-catching but easily tarnished and expensive metal chiefly used at formal dinner parties as an aid in turning the conversation toward the servant problem, the crime problem, and the inflation problem.
Simmer	To cook a liquid mixture at a temperature just high enough to cause a thick layer of food to become welded to the bottom of the pan, but low enough to ensure that the remainder will be too thin and watery to be used as a soup, stew, or sauce.
Sink	A stain into which a steady drip passes on its way to a clog.
Skim	*1.* To remove scum or fat from the surface of (a liquid). *2.* To read through (a recipe) in so cursory a fashion that one does not notice the warning that unless the scum or fat is removed from the surface of the liquid, the resulting dish will taste like a gym bag.

Soufflé Delectable but very demanding baked dish that is quite susceptible to collapse in the oven. Because of its tendency to shatter the hopes and ruin the demeanor of even the most stoical cook, the soufflé is familiarly known among pastry chefs as the Snifflé, the Snufflé, the Soboise, and the Boue-houe.

Southern Cooking American regional cuisine featuring dishes like hush puppies, hoppin' john, hominy grits, okra gumbo, chitlins, po' boys, potlikker, and pone. Cooks without roots in the Deep South rarely serve these unique foods, and that is a serious culinary omission since the occasional presentation of an authentic southern meal gives the home chef the option at a later date of announcing an accidentally burned heap of black, greasy, crusted goo as the traditional Gulf Coast treat, Fuddah, Crudlins, Po' Nuff, and Mumble Grunny, with Spacklins and Shmuh.

Spinach Incredibly enough, this revolting leafy vegetable has been found to contain large amounts of oxalic acid, a substance that hinders the absorption of calcium and iron and can, in large quantities, actually be poisonous. To counteract its potentially deleterious effects, one can either consume additional skim milk and liver or cut way down on the amount of spinach ingested. (Persons unsure of which nutritional choice to make are urged to greatly increase their intake of fish, a legendary brain food.)

Spoon Basic kitchen implement. Spoons of all sizes are used in cooking, but recipe amounts always refer to the standard teaspoon (tsp.) and tablespoon (tbsp.) found in a set of special measuring spoons. Still, many cooks use any odd spoon that comes to hand and determine the volume of salt, spices, and the like to add to a particular dish

Spoon

Timer

according to a more casual calculation of quantity such as the heaping soupspoon (tsk.), the half-full ladle (trbl.), and the level ice-cream scoop (trgdy.).

Steak A slice of meat from the short loin of beef. The most popular steak in America in terms of quantity sold is a cut consisting of the top loin, the tenderloin, and a portion of the flank or tail. This used to be called the porterhouse, but following the considerable increase in meat prices over the last two decades is now more commonly known as the poorhouse, the nuthouse, or the mortgagehouse.

Sugar One of a class of carbohydrates present in one form or another in all foods. Common sources of sugar and the types they contain are: fructose and glucose (fruit juice and honey); lactose (milk); sucrose (sugar cane or sugar beets); maltose (malt); and jocose, verbose, morose, lachrymose, bellicose, and comatose (alcohol).

Supermarket Very large, well-stocked food store that sells both spoiled fruit and the wrong-size flashlight battery.

T

Tapioca The only known dessert that produces leftovers.

Taste *1.* The ability to distinguish between, say, tripes à la mode de Caen and chocolate pudding. *2.* The critical discernment necessary to choose the chocolate pudding.

Tie *See* GRAVY.

Timer Adjustable clock that rings or otherwise signals when a particular dish is overcooked.

Toaster

Countertop appliance for browning bread. Toasters vary somewhat in design, but all modern units have a dial for selecting any setting from "char" to "incinerate"; a special crumb dump in which bits of bread are held until they are gradually transformed into coal; a special dimmer that reduces lighting throughout the house to a soft, romantic glow while toast is cooking; a self-locking slide mechanism that keeps slices from being raised until they are fully carbonized; a 17-foot cord; and an unconditional 10-minute or 10-slice warranty.

Tofu

Soybean curd favored by health food enthusiasts. It is dense and colorless and has very little taste, proving the truth of the adage that you are what you eat.

Tomato

Although this very popular foodstuff is, botanically speaking, a fruit, the Supreme Court in 1893 declared it to be a vegetable. Since that historic decision, the highest court in the land has come to regret its intervention in strictly culinary matters as it quickly was called upon to settle a number of bothersome lawsuits, including petitions to declare saltwater taffy unconstitutional as an interference in free speech (1926); find that garlic restricted freedom of assembly (1934); intern sukiyaki and tempura (1942); rule on the inclusion of loyalty oaths in imported fortune cookies (1952); consider whether serving beans to an accused murderer held without bail during his trial violated his right to remain silent (1959); decide whether oysters suspected of contamination could be opened without a search warrant (1965); and judge whether minorities were excluded from wine- and cheese-tasting panels (1973).

Tongue

A variety meat, not much served because it clearly crosses the line between a cut of beef and a piece of dead cow.

Toaster
A
B
C
D
E
F
G
H
I

Utensil

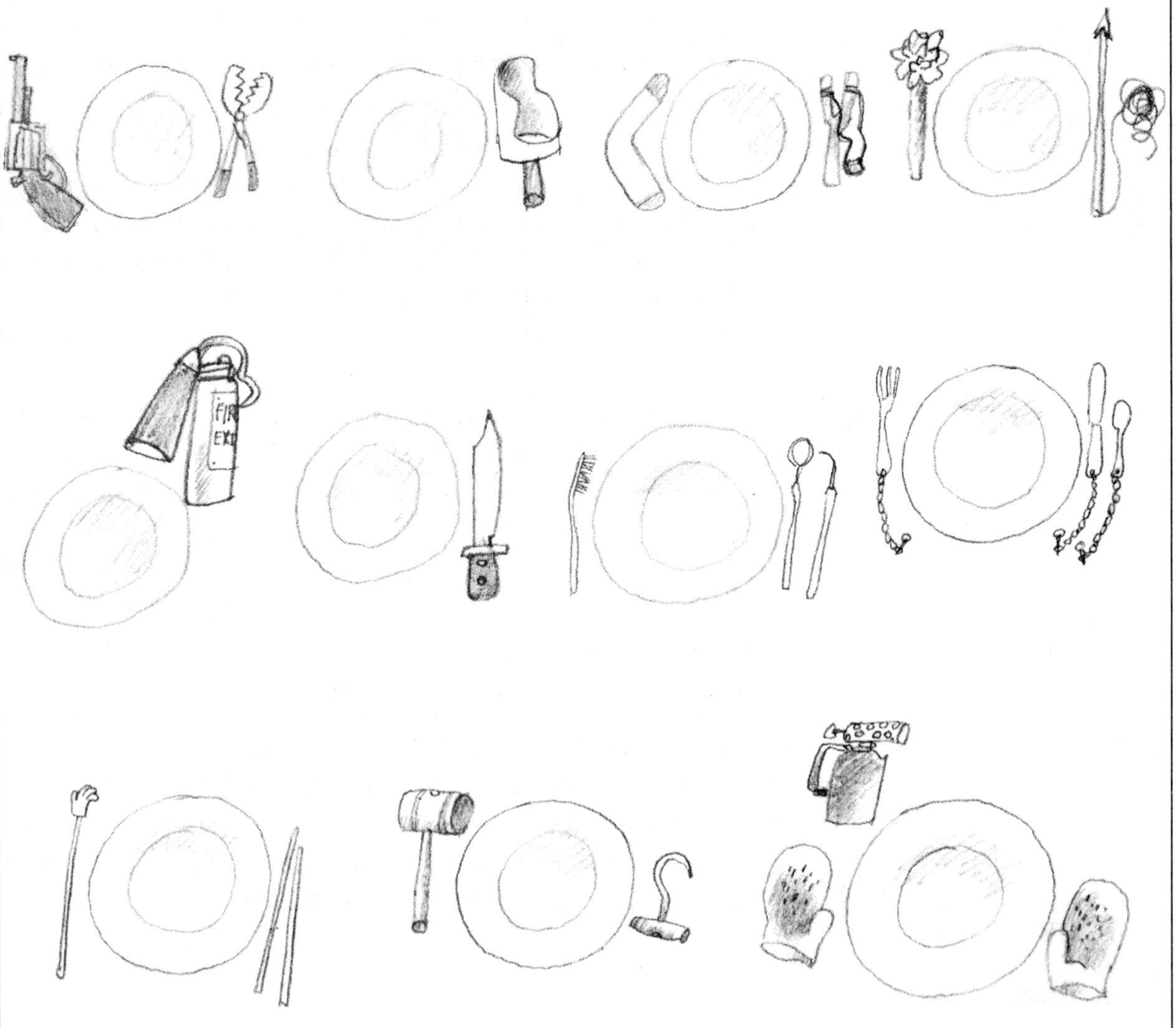

Tray A portable mess.

Turkey Large, domesticated game bird native to North America. Turkey is intimately linked in American minds with Thanksgiving, a holiday that celebrates the feast held in 1621 at Plymouth Colony between the Pilgrims and Chief Massasoit of the Wampanoags. Massasoit, who favored peace with the European settlers, brought turkey, goose, venison, and various fruits and berries. His canny brother, Succotash, who hated and feared the colonists and hoped to encourage them to go back home by convincing them that New World food was unspeakable, brought the corn-and-lima bean dish that bears his name to this day, as well as chipped buffalo on corn bread, squash slaw, a beer brewed from thistles, codfish mush, beet stew, boiled turnips, chokecherry pie, deer liver and leeks, and eel wine. Flabbergasted when the hungry Puritans greedily devoured his most loathsome concoctions, he went mad and spent the rest of his days going from settlement to settlement in odd get-ups, howling, chanting, and mumbling. He is thus regarded as the spiritual father both of New England cooking and of summer-stock theater.

Turnip Nasty root vegetable. Turnip-eating contests are occasionally held, and the current world record for the largest number of turnips eaten at a single sitting is two, although persons inclined to disbelieve this incredible figure insist they must have been unusually small ones.

U

Utensil A spill, cut, burn, or bungle with a handle on the end.

V

Veal

Tender, delicately flavored meat of a young calf, most often sold as scaloppine, i.e., cutlets pounded flat for sautéing. If the butcher has pounded the cutlets to less than one-sixteenth of an inch of thickness, they should technically be labeled wallopine. Also, unscrupulous markets have occasionally been known to substitute horsemeat for veal. Beware of any meat marketed as veal gallopine.

Vegetarian

Individual who declines to eat animal products, on either moral or nutritional grounds. Since vegetarians are often inclined to be somewhat self-righteous in the presence of meat-eaters, people who consume beef and poultry relish encounters between vegetarians and the considerably more fervent mineralarians, who shun both animal and vegetable matter. Because their meals of marl, rutile, and bentonite, with maybe a simple salad of red clay, peat, and feldspar, make these dietary fanatics quite testy, they can be counted on to attack vegetarians as "herbicidal maniacs" and "sap-thirsty cutstems" whose hands are stained green from a gruesome harvest of defenseless plant life.

Vinaigrette

Basic French dressing that consists of too much oil added a bit too quickly to a mixture containing partially ground peppercorns from a malfunctioning mill, an excess of salt, all the juice that could be gotten out of an old lemon half, and dry mustard that fell out of the can in a big lump.

Vinegar

Sour liquid made chiefly from fermented wine or cider and used as a flavoring, particularly in salad dressings. In recent years, purveyors of fancy foods have transformed vinegar, and to some degree mustard, into gourmet food products

Vegetarian

Whisk

with the addition of peppercorns, fennel, dill, thyme, and so forth. Those who hoped that this pointless fad would pass will not be cheered to learn that in the coming year major food conglomerates plan to introduce shallot-tarragon tartar sauce, herb Tabasco, and basil ketchup.

Vitamins

The major vitamins, a few of their sources, and some of their recognized effects are: A (carrots and other root vegetables), physical growth, healthy eyes and skin; B-1 (cereals, pork, legumes), healthy nerves, good digestion; B-2 (dairy products, eggs, liver), good metabolism, proper muscular function; niacin (lean meat, cereal, liver), healthy skin; B-12 (seafood, dairy products), blood-cell formation; C (citrus fruits), healthy gums and teeth; D (oily fish and eggs), proper bone growth; E (vegetable oils), muscle tone, fertility; and K (rice, bran), blood clotting. In addition, dedicated nutrition nuts believe in the existence and consume large amounts of the following unrecognized vitamins: L (fruit pits, corn cobs), lush beard growth, fixed toothy smile; Q (bean curd, fish meal), piercing eyes, unnerving stare; X (nut husks, kelp, bark), bone-crushing handshake; Y (pumpkin stems), tireless tongue, long wind; and Z (beet greens, millet), thick skull, bony head.

W

Whisk

One of a number of exercise devices used by sedentary cooks to develop muscles and improve body tone. Other items of workout equipment found in kitchens include the eggbeater (strengthens pectorals), the cheese grater (enlarges triceps), and the salad spinner (firms up deltoids).

Wine The characteristics of wine of interest to connoisseurs and the words used to describe them are aroma (bouquet, nose, vinosity, fragrance); flavor (depth, earthy, full, subtle); character (big, round, body, rich, buttery, balanced); and aftertaste (length, finish, départ). On the other hand, the qualities given most weight by cooks planning a dinner as they examine the offerings in their local liquor store are coloration (red, white, rosé, and other); cost (bite, hit, insult, sting, clip, squeeze); and ability of the label to impress (push, cut, curl, shoulder, lip, mouth, and cheek).

Wok Large, round-bottomed frying pan used in cooking Chinese dishes. Several other pieces of Oriental culinary equipment are employed in the preparation of Chinese food, including special implements for stir-frying, Chinese cleavers, cook's chopsticks, and a bamboo brush for cleaning the wok, but there is no need to purchase any of these utensils since every kitchen already has a handy wall-mounted device with a rotary dial or push buttons with which it is possible to produce a complete Chinese meal within three-quarters of an hour in most urban and suburban areas.

X

Xeres Town in the Andalusian province of Spain from which sherry—a corruption of its name—originally came. Sherry is the liquor most commonly used in cooking, followed in popularity by red and white wine, but virtually any alcoholic beverage can add flavor to a dish, and the choice really depends on whether the food is being marinated, simmered, sautéed, or flambéed, and whether the cook is to be oiled, pickled, fried, or stewed.

Yeast

Y

Yeast

One-celled fungus which, through fermentation, converts sugar into two by-products: alcohol, thereby making beer, whiskey, and wine possible; and carbon dioxide, which causes cakes and pastry to rise and become light and delicate. Thus, incredibly enough, one tiny microscopic organism is responsible for both drinks and dessert. Recognizing this awesome power to convert unpromising ingredients into valuable foodstuffs, scientists have been at work for some time using gene splicing, cloning, and RNA/DNA transfer techniques to develop new strains that could, for example, metabolize remaindered diet books into a cheap animal feed; change hominy grits into anything else, even dog food; and transmute creamed chicken into something useful, like tub caulk or window putty.

Yogurt

Semisolid dairy product made from partly evaporated and fermented milk. Yogurt is one of only three foods that taste exactly the same as they sound. The other two are goulash and squid.

Z

Zinfandel

Red wine produced in very large volume in California and available by the liter or gallon in both premium and unleaded varieties. The best recent vintage is the 11:35 A.M., though some people swear by the 9:58.